Delia Smith's Cookery Course Part Three

Delia Smith's Cookery Course

Part Three

BRITISH BROADCASTING CORPORATION

This book accompanies the third part of the
BBC Television series *Delia Smith's Cookery Course*
Part three of this series first broadcast on BBC-2
from April 1981. Producer: Peter Riding

Photographs by Bob Komar
Drawings by Ray and Corrine Burrows
Food preparation for photography by Elaine Bastable

Grateful thanks to Elaine Bastable, Linda Blakemore,
Susan Goodman, Elisabeth Ingham, Alison Leach,
Stuart Morris, Gwyneth Phillips and Rosemary Oates
for their help in the preparation of this book

Acknowledgment is due to Universal Pictorial Press
and Agency for the portrait of Delia Smith on the cover
The BBC would also like to thank the following for
the loan of equipment and accessories for the photographs:
Divertimenti, Marylebone Lane, London W1
Selfridges Limited, Oxford Street, London W1

Published to accompany a series of programmes prepared in
consultation with the BBC Continuing Education Advisory Council

First published 1981. Reprinted 1981 (twice)
Published by the British Broadcasting Corporation
35 Marylebone High Street, London W1M 4AA
ISBN 0 563 16456 5

Filmset in 12/13 point Baskerville
Printed and bound in Great Britain by Mackays of Chatham Ltd
and Balding and Mansell Limited, Wisbech, Cambridgeshire

Contents

Conversion tables

All these are *approximate* conversions, which have either been rounded up or down. In a few recipes it has been necessary to modify them very slightly. Never mix metric and imperial measures in one recipe, stick to one system or the other. All spoon measurements used throughout this book are level unless specified otherwise.

Oven temperatures

Mark 1	275°F	140°C
2	300	150
3	325	170
4	350	180
5	375	190
6	400	200
7	425	220
8	450	230
9	475	240

Volume

2 fl oz	55 ml
3	75
5 ($\frac{1}{4}$ pt)	150
10 ($\frac{1}{2}$ pt)	275
15 ($\frac{3}{4}$ pt)	425
20 (1 pt)	570
$1\frac{3}{4}$ pt	1 litre

Measurements

$\frac{1}{8}$ inch	3 mm
$\frac{1}{4}$	$\frac{1}{2}$ cm
$\frac{1}{2}$	1
$\frac{3}{4}$	2
1	2·5
$1\frac{1}{4}$	3
$1\frac{1}{2}$	4
$1\frac{3}{4}$	4·5
2	5
3	7·5
4	10
5	13
6	15
7	18
8	20
9	23
10	25·5
11	28
12	30

Weights

$\frac{1}{2}$ oz	10 g
1	25
$1\frac{1}{2}$	40
2	50
$2\frac{1}{2}$	60
3	75
4	110
$4\frac{1}{2}$	125
5	150
6	175
7	200
8	225
9	250
10	275
12	350
1 lb	450
$1\frac{1}{2}$ lb	700
2 lb	900
3 lb	1 kg 350 g

Introduction

This is the third, and final, instalment of the Cookery Course.
I said at the beginning of the whole project (three years ago!)
that I hoped the Course, when completed, would give beginners a
grasp of the basics of everyday cooking and, perhaps some new
inspiration to more experienced cooks. Your letters and reactions
to the first two series—which have been of enormous help to
me—suggest that the books and the programmes have indeed
been of practical value, and Part Three has been written with
precisely the same aims in mind, though with more of a flavour
of spring and summer.

That is not to say there isn't plenty left to say on the subject of
cooking, of course. It is an endless process: the more one cooks, the
more one learns. Personally I have learned a tremendous amount
researching for and writing these books, and one of the most
important things perhaps is that there is no definitive method of
cooking. The Cookery Course, really, is a set of guidelines which
I have found work best for me (and I sincerely hope for you too).
You'll always find people who say something *must* be done in
such-and-such a way and no other; and commercial concerns who
say that they produce the products we want are actually trying to
persuade us to want the products they produce. (Several of them
have taken me to task for saying in the Cookery Course that
certain foods, or methods of production, lack flavour.) The fact is,
there is no scientific substitute for *experience* of cooking and eating:
it may be a hackneyed saying but the proof of the pudding, or the
cake or casserole, *is* in the eating.

Another conclusion I have drawn from fifteen years of cooking
and writing about food is—people are more important than food.
It is all very well for chefs in grand kitchens to dedicate themselves
to haute cuisine and all its complications, because they don't have
to serve and eat it later and mingle with the guests. You and I,
when we entertain, have to play the dual role of cook and host, and
nothing can turn a meal (however good it is) to ashes faster than a
flustered cook who transmits his or her panic to the guests. I like to
concentrate, therefore, on flavour rather than effect, to serve meals
that need as little last-minute attention as possible, and to try to
please people rather than dazzle them.

Inevitably, I suppose, there will be omissions of some kind in
the Cookery Course. And for those I apologise in advance, though

in the space available to me I have tried to cover what I consider to be the most important areas. I have had a number of requests to include information on freezing food in the Course, for example. But freezing is not cooking, in fact it is a large and complex subject on its own. Owning a freezer seems to dictate a way of life which is not always compatible with my own philosophy of food—that is to buy and cook fresh foods when they are in season. However for those who already use, or are planning to buy, a freezer there are plenty of specialist books on the market. If this Cookery Course has proved to anyone that cooking need not be difficult, that it can actually be a lot of fun, I shall be more than happy.

Delia Smith

Advanced pastry and cakes

Including recipes for:

Home baking and pastry-making are coming back into our lives, I feel. And it is largely because so many of those 'home-made' and highly individual corner bakers are disappearing under the pressure of the big factory chains. True, a family baking session has to be fitted into busy schedules—when the best is usually the quickest, and the pastries we discussed earlier in the Course, like shortcrust and quick flaky pastry, are ideal for such occasions.

However, there are times when we can embark on baking just for our own pleasure and satisfaction—or when an occasion calls for something rather special. This is what this chapter is about. But don't be put off by the word 'advanced'. The pastry and cake recipes are *not* difficult, but they do take a little more time, and you need to allow for this. I would never, for instance, make my own puff pastry when I'm under pressure at Christmas-time, because there are so many other things to do. But when you have the time and space to give your mind to it, there is no treat quite like your own home-made puff pastry, which has a crispness and flavour the frozen kind can never match.

First let's look at a pastry which some people—mistakenly I think—find rather daunting: the famous French choux pastry.

Choux pastry

This is the light, crisp, airy pastry which is used to make éclairs, profiteroles, or savoury gougères. It puffs up in the oven until it is eventually set by the heat of the cooking. The airiness, in fact, is caused because choux has a high water content, which in cooking is turned into steam, which forces the pastry shell outwards, and gives it some volume.

What's so good about choux is that it doesn't call for any particular pastry skills (like lightness of hand or careful rolling). Of course some people make hard work of it by recommending that it always has to be piped through piping bags. But personally —quite apart from the fact that piping requires experience and a steady hand—I find it a wasteful method; and I'm convinced that a freshly-baked golden profiterole looks so much crustier if it's spooned, rather than piped, onto a baking sheet.

My own advice on choux pastry can be summarised as follows:

Try to use strong plain flour, which (with its higher gluten content) gives crisper results than ordinary soft plain flour.

Raising the oven temperature during the cooking, I have found, gives really crisp, well-risen choux.

Choux pastry doesn't keep well, and it is best eaten as soon as possible. It will stay crisp for up to 4 hours, though I prefer to have mine ready just 2 hours before it is needed.

Fillings, if put in too far in advance, make the pastry soggy. So it is advisable to fill the cakes, buns or whatever as near as possible to the time they are to be eaten.

Basic choux pastry	
	2½ oz strong plain flour (60 g)
	2 oz butter, cut into small pieces (50 g)
	1 teaspoon sugar (only for sweet choux pastry, otherwise use a seasoning of salt and pepper)
	2 eggs, well beaten
	5 fl oz cold water (150 ml)

Pre-heat the oven to gas mark 6, 400°F (200°C)

First of all, put the water in a medium-sized saucepan together with the pieces of butter, and leave on one side while you weigh out the flour.

As you are going to need to 'shoot' the flour quickly into the water and melted butter, fold a sheet of greaseproof paper to make a crease, then open it up again. Sift the flour straight onto the square of greaseproof. If the end product is going to be sweet, add a teaspoon of sugar to the flour; if it is to be savoury, season the flour well with salt and pepper instead.

Next, place the saucepan of water and butter over a moderate heat, and stir with a wooden spoon. As soon as the butter has melted and the mixture comes up to the boil, turn off the heat and tip the flour in—all in one go—with one hand, while you beat the mixture vigorously with the other (you can do this with a wooden spoon, though an electric hand-whisk will save you lots of energy).

Beat until you have a smooth ball of paste that has left the sides of the saucepan clean (probably this will take less than a minute). Then beat the beaten eggs in—a little at a time—until you have a smooth glossy paste.

At this stage grease a baking sheet lightly, then hold it under cold running water for a few seconds, and tap it sharply to get rid of excess moisture (this will help create a steamy atmosphere, which in turn helps the pastry to rise). Your choux pastry is then ready for any of the following recipes.

Gougère with cheese

(serves 2 people)

This is a ring of cheese-flavoured choux pastry, crisp on the outside and slightly squidgy inside. It is nice served with a salad for a lunch dish.

1 quantity of choux pastry (see page 491)
2½ oz Cheddar cheese, grated (60 g)
½ teaspoon mustard powder
A good pinch cayenne pepper
Salt and freshly-milled black pepper to season

Pre-heat the oven to gas mark 6, 400°F (200°C)

Make the choux paste in exactly the same way as outlined on page 491—seasoning with salt and pepper—except that immediately after you have added the beaten eggs, also add 2 oz (50 g) of the cheese, the mustard and the cayenne pepper.

Now spoon dessertspoonfuls of the mixture onto a greased and ready-dampened baking sheet, so that they touch each other and form a circle that is approximately 7 inches (18 cm) in diameter.

Brush the choux circle with some beaten egg, then sprinkle the remaining grated cheese all round the top. Bake in the pre-heated oven for 10 minutes, then increase the heat to gas mark 7, 425°F (220°C) and cook for a further 20–25 minutes. Serve it hot and puffy, straight from the oven.

Note: to make this recipe extra special, you could use Swiss gruyère cheese instead of Cheddar.

Profiteroles

(makes about 18)

Profiteroles—little choux buns filled with cream and covered in a chocolate sauce—make a rather special ending to a dinner party.

1 quantity choux pastry (see page 491)
½ pint double cream, whipped thick (275 ml)
½ lb plain chocolate (225 g)
3 tablespoons water

1 large baking sheet, greased and dampened

Pre-heat the oven to gas mark 6, 400°F (200°C)

Place teaspoonfuls of choux paste on the baking sheet, and then bake in the pre-heated oven for 10 minutes. After that, increase the heat to gas mark 7, 425°F (220°C) and bake for a further 15–20 minutes until the choux buns are crisp, light and a rich golden colour. Pierce the side of each one (to let out the steam), then cool them on a wire rack.

To make the chocolate sauce, melt the chocolate together with the water in a basin fitted over a saucepan of simmering water, stirring until you have a smooth sauce (see my note on chocolate, page 680). Just before serving, split the choux buns in half, fill each one with a teaspoonful of whipped cream, then join the halves together again. Pour the melted chocolate over them (see the photograph on page 687) and serve immediately.

Note: don't be tempted to put the cream in too far in advance, because this tends to make them soggy.

Chocolate and hazelnut choux buns

(makes 8 or 9)

These lovely, light airy choux buns are filled and topped with a squidgy chocolate mousse mixture and coated with chopped nuts.

1 quantity of choux pastry (see page 491)

For the filling:
6 oz plain dessert chocolate (175 g)
3 large eggs, separated

For the topping:
2 level tablespoons chopped, toasted hazelnuts

The mousse filling should be made several hours in advance. Melt the chocolate in a heat-proof bowl set over a pan of barely simmering water. Then beat the egg yolks into the chocolate and allow the mixture to cool. Whisk the egg whites to the soft peak stage. Stir one tablespoon of egg white into the chocolate mixture to loosen it, then carefully fold in the remainder. Cover the bowl and chill in a refrigerator for about 3 hours.

Pre-heat the oven to gas mark 6, 400°F (200°C). Place rough dessertspoonfuls of the choux pastry on a greased and dampened baking sheet and bake, on a high shelf, for 10 minutes. Then increase the heat to gas mark 7, 425°F (220°C) for a further 20–25 minutes until the buns are nicely brown and puffy. Pierce the side of each one and cool on a wire cooling tray.

It's best not to put in the filling until about an hour before serving. All you do is slice the choux buns horizontally, but not quite in half, then place a spoonful of the chocolate mousse inside, spread a little over the top using the back of the spoon and, finally, sprinkle each one with chopped hazelnuts.

Coffee éclairs
(makes 8 or 9)

You can, of course, make these as the choux buns in the last recipe but if you want to serve the classic éclair shape, you'll need to use a piping bag.

1 quantity of choux pastry (see page 491)

For the filling:
½ pint double cream (275 ml)
1 tablespoon instant coffee
2 teaspoons boiling water
1 tablespoon caster sugar

For the icing:
5 oz sieved icing sugar (150 g)
2 teaspoons instant coffee
1 tablespoon boiling water

Pre-heat the oven to gas mark 6, 400°F (200°C)

Spoon the choux pastry into a large nylon piping bag, fitted with a plain ½ inch (1 cm) piping nozzle. Pipe the mixture onto rinsed baking sheets (see the recipe on page 491) in lengths just over 3 inches (7·5 cm).

Bake the éclairs on a high shelf for 10 minutes, then increase the heat to gas mark 7, 425°F (220°C) for a further 10 minutes. Remove them from the oven to a wire cooling tray and make a slight hole in the side of each one.

For the filling, dissolve the coffee and sugar in the boiling water. Beat the cream till thickened and add the coffee mixture to it, stirring to blend it evenly. Now wash and dry the piping bag and nozzle thoroughly; spoon the coffee cream into it. Slit the éclairs along one side, pipe in the cream and carefully press the tops gently back over the cream.

Next prepare the icing. In a small basin dissolve the coffee in the boiling water, sift the icing sugar into it and stir. It should now be the consistency of thick cream. Finally, dip the tops of the éclairs into the icing and let the excess drip back into the bowl before returning each one to the wire rack.

Note: as an alternative filling for choux buns, profiteroles or éclairs you could use the *Crème patisserie* on page 501. For coffee flavour, add 1 dessertspoon of instant coffee dissolved in 1 teaspoon warm water and for a chocolate filling, combine the cream with 2 oz (50 g) melted dessert chocolate.

Puff Pastry

Some time ago I had almost given up on home-made puff pastry. It wasn't that I couldn't make it well, it was just that I couldn't spare the *time* to make it well! All that long resting and rolling never seemed to fit in with the rest of my life, and I would either leave it too long in the fridge (so that I couldn't roll it), or I would be impatient and not leave it long enough.

Then, a few years ago, my friend John Tovey showed me his method, which takes 30 minutes flat. Because his is the best I've ever tasted (invariably light and crisp), I no longer persevere with any of the other methods. His recipe follows, but first some general points about puff pastry.

What is puff pastry? It is the pastry used for vol-au-vents, sausage rolls, mince pies, jam puffs, and toppings for savoury and fruit pies. Unlike shortcrust or suet crust pastries, both of which can be described as granular in texture, puff pastry is made up of a number of thin layers (although they're close together, they are in fact quite separate). This is achieved by layering the fat into the flour, rather than rubbing it in. The dough is also folded (more layering), and after folding sealed at the edges, so that air is trapped inside. During the baking the expansion of steam forces the layers up, and the pastry rises (hence the French name for puff pastries, *mille feuilles* or thousand leaves).

Finally a few points to bear in mind when making puff pastry:

Always use strong flour.

The fat should be at room temperature when making the pastry, but the finished pastry should be thoroughly chilled before using (preferably overnight).

Allow the pastry to come back to room temperature before rolling out for use.

Once rolled and cut out, the pastry should be allowed to chill again (15–20 minutes) before going into the oven.

Dampen the baking sheet with cold water—to create a steamy atmosphere in the oven which encourages the pastry to rise.

The oven *must* be hot: gas mark 8, 450°F (230°C). Use the shelf just above the centre of the oven.

Warning! Having assembled a quantity of beautifully layered puff pastry, remember that the trimmings you have left after rolling out and cutting will not be layered together laterally. So re-rolled trimmings will not rise up and layer in quite the same way as the pastry from the first rolling. I think it is best to keep the trimmings (in a polythene bag in the fridge) for later use as a pie crust or for *Richmond maids of honour* (see page 500).

John Tovey's rough puff pastry

This, unlike my quick flaky pastry earlier in the Course, is the real thing—perfect, puffy, flaky layers, which are very light and crisp.

1 lb strong plain flour, sifted with a pinch of salt (450 g)

8 oz margarine (225 g), cut into ½ oz (10 g) pieces (i.e. 16 pieces)
8 oz lard (225 g), cut into ½ oz (10 g) pieces
½ pint iced water (275 ml), less 1 tablespoon
1 tablespoon lemon juice

Sift the flour and salt into a bowl, then add the pieces of fat. Now just flick them around to get them all coated with flour, but don't 'work' the pastry yet or attempt to mix them in. Make a well in the centre and pour in the iced water mixed with the lemon juice. Take a palette knife and make cuts across and across, turning the bowl around as you go so that you gently bring all the ingredients together. Work quickly, and as soon as you have a reasonable lump of mixture, turn it out onto a floured board—along with all the loose flour that's left.

Now, using your hands, lightly and gently shape the mixture into a brick shape, then take a large, long rolling-pin and (holding it right at the ends) make three quick depressions widthwise, to trap the air. Then, still keeping your hands at the ends of the pin (the pressure should not be directly over the pastry) roll the brick shape into an oblong roughly 13 inches (32·5 cm) long and 8 inches (20 cm) wide.

Fold one-third over to the centre, then the other third over that. Use your pin to press the edges firmly and again trap the air. Now rest the pastry for 5 minutes, then lift it and flour the board. Give the pastry a quick quarter-turn and make three depressions again. Repeat the whole process three more times, remembering to keep your board and pin well floured throughout. Wrap the pastry in foil or polythene and chill well before using, preferably overnight.

Note: before attempting to roll the pastry out for use, do make sure you allow it to come back to room temperature.

Vol-au-vents
Traditional vol-au-vents are rather fiddly things to make: they require a certain thickness of pastry to make room for the fillings, and then quite a bit of the soggy centre has to be scraped out and wasted. John Tovey has come up with the brilliant idea of simply baking small rounds of pastry, halving them, and sandwiching them together with a filling. The results are far crisper, with less pastry and more filling—a lighter, tastier product altogether.

Basic
vol-au-vents
(makes 12)

1 lb John Tovey's rough puff pastry (half the quantity on pages 496–497)

Pre-heat the oven to gas mark 8, 450°F (230°C)

Roll the pastry out to about ⅛ inch (3 mm) thick as evenly as possible, then using a 3½ inch (8·5 cm) fluted cutter cut out twelve rounds. Place these on a damp baking sheet, and leave them to rest for 10 minutes in a cool place or in the fridge. Brush each one with a little milk or beaten egg, and bake on a high shelf in the oven for 10–15 minutes.

When they are a good rich golden colour, remove them from the oven and transfer to a wire cooling tray. Slice each one in half horizontally (making sure you keep them in pairs, ready for re-assembling). If there is any uncooked pastry in the centre, scrape it out—but there should be only very little.

If you use the hot mushroom filling (see following recipe) you can fill and serve the vol-au-vents straightaway, or else warm them through and fill when you are ready. For cold fillings such as the cream cheese one on the next page, fill and sandwich them together just before serving.

You can serve the vol-au-vents as a lunch-time snack with a salad (2 per person) or as a first course (1–2 per person). For buffet parties, or for serving with drinks, you can make small, bite-sized versions, using a 2 inch (5 cm) cutter. Remember that they shrink in width during cooking.

Note: for the hot vol-au-vents, a little melted butter brushed over the surface before serving gives them a lovely sheen.

Hot mushroom
and bacon filling

2 oz butter (50 g)
Half a medium-sized onion, chopped fairly small
2 rashers back bacon, chopped
1 oz flour (25 g)
8 oz mushrooms, roughly chopped (225 g)
8 fl oz single cream (220 ml)
Freshly grated nutmeg
Salt and freshly-milled black pepper

Melt the butter gently in a pan, and soften the onion and bacon in it for about 5 minutes. Then stir in the mushrooms and cook over a gentle heat for about 6 more minutes, stirring now and then. Next sprinkle in the flour, and stir well to soak up all the juices. Add the cream, a little at a time, stirring well after each addition. Cook the mixture for about 5 minutes (still giving it the odd stir). Taste and season with as much salt, pepper and nutmeg as you think it needs. Finally spoon the filling onto the warm vol-au-vents and sandwich them together.

Cream cheese and herb filling

6 oz cream cheese (225 g)
2 cloves garlic, crushed
2 tablespoons finely chopped parsley
2 tablespoons snipped chives
Salt and freshly-milled black pepper

Simply mash the ingredients together, blending them thoroughly. Taste to check the seasoning, then use the mixture to sandwich the cold vol-au-vents together (being fairly generous with the filling) just before serving.

Cream puffs
(makes 12)

These are a sweet 'afternoon tea' version of the basic vol-au-vent recipe.

1 lb John Tovey's rough puff pastry (half the quantity on pages 496–497)
2 tablespoons granulated sugar
A little milk

For the filling:
6 heaped teaspoons strawberry jam (or any other flavour)
5 fl oz (150 ml) whipped cream

Pre-heat the oven to gas mark 8, 450°F (230°C)

Roll and cut the pastry as in the basic recipe on page 498. Brush each round on one side with milk, place it milk-side down on a saucer of granulated sugar, then bake them on a baking sheet (sugar-side uppermost) to get a nice, sugary, crusty topping.

Bake on a high shelf in the oven for 10 to 15 minutes, then split them, cool and sandwich together with jam and whipped cream. If you don't want to bother with a sugar-crusted topping, leave them plain and simply dust them with icing sugar before serving.

Richmond maids of honour

(makes about 16)

These little puff pastry cheese cakes were said to have been created by the maids of honour at Richmond Palace in the 16th century.

8 oz puff pastry (225 g), (quarter the quantity on pages 496–497)
A little apricot jam
8 oz curd cheese (225 g), (or cottage cheese sieved)
1 large egg
1 extra yolk
1½ oz caster sugar (40 g)
The grated rind of 1 lemon
1 oz ground almonds (25 g)
1 rounded tablespoon currants
A little icing sugar

Pre-heat the oven to gas mark 6, 400°F (200°C)

Start by rolling out the pastry to ⅛ inch (3 mm) thick, then using a 3¼ inch (8 cm) fluted cutter cut out little circles and place them in tartlet tins.

Combine the cheese, caster sugar, lemon rind, ground almonds and currants in a bowl, then beat the egg and egg yolk together and add this as well. Mix, very thoroughly, with a fork until everything is evenly blended. Next, spoon the merest trace of jam into the base of each pastry case, and fill each one about two-thirds full with the cheese mixture. Bake them in the centre of the oven for about 25–30 minutes by which time the mixture will have puffed right up and turned a lovely golden brown.

Take them out of the oven and transfer them onto a wire rack to cool. Don't worry as you see the centres starting to sink down because that's absolutely correct and normal. When they're cool they'll look nice with a faint dusting of icing sugar sifted over.

Crème patisserie
(makes 15 fl oz)

This delicious custard cream makes an alternative—almost better—filling than fresh cream for all kinds of pastries.

15 fl oz milk (425 ml)
1 vanilla pod
4 oz caster sugar (110 g)
5 egg yolks
2 level tablespoons plain flour
1 level tablespoon cornflour
½ oz butter (10 g)

Pour the milk into a pan, and pop in the vanilla pod. Bring to the boil, then take the pan off the heat and leave for the milk to infuse.

Whisk the egg yolks together with the caster sugar in a bowl, until the mixture is thick and creamy-coloured. Then gradually whisk in the flour and the cornflour. Remove the vanilla pod from the milk, and pour the infused milk into the egg yolk mixture—stirring vigorously as you pour. Return the whole lot to the rinsed-out pan and bring to the boil over a medium heat (still stirring all the time). Simmer for 3 minutes and continue to beat briskly. As the mixture thickens lumps may form, but these will eventually beat out. Take the pan off the heat, and finally beat in the butter. Transfer the cream to a bowl, and cover closely with a buttered sheet of greaseproof paper over the surface, to prevent a skin forming. Leave to get cold—but use the cream within 2–3 days.

Note: after the cream has thickened you could add a little liqueur!

Rich flan pastry
I like a light, crunchy, nutty-flavoured pastry for 'special' open fruit flans. When making either of the two recipes that follow, I make a 6 oz (175 g) quantity of pastry which is enough to line an 8 inch (20 cm) flan tin and also make a lattice-work top.

Crisp cinnamon flan
(serves 6 people)

6 oz plain flour (175 g)
3 oz butter (75 g)
3 tablespoons caster sugar
3 egg yolks
1 teaspoon cinnamon

For the filling:

1 lb blackcurrants, gooseberries or loganberries (450 g)

2 tablespoons granulated sugar

1 rounded teaspoon arrowroot

A little caster sugar for decorating

An 8 inch (20 cm) flan tin, lightly greased

Pre-heat the oven to gas mark 6, 400°F (200°C)

First prepare the pastry. Sieve the flour with the cinnamon into a mixing bowl, then rub in the fat, stir in the sugar and use the egg yolks in place of liquid to mix the pastry to a dough. Pop it into a polythene bag and chill for one hour in the fridge before using.

Meanwhile prepare the filling, by sprinkling the sugar over the fruit in a saucepan and heating gently until the juice begins to run. Then mix the arrowroot with enough cold water to make a smooth paste, mix this with the fruit and simmer till thickened.

To make the flan, roll out three-quarters of the pastry and line the flan tin with it, pricking the base with a fork. Now fill with the fruit mixture and arrange the remaining pastry in a lattice pattern over the top. Brush the top with cold water, dust with a little caster sugar, then bake on a baking sheet for 10 minutes. Reduce the heat to gas mark 5, 375°F (190°C) and cook for a further 35 minutes. Serve (warm or cold) with whipped cream.

Linzertorte

(serves 6 people)

This is a famous Austrian torte named after the town of Linz. The rich pastry flan is made with ground hazelnuts. If you can't get hold of cranberry jelly, redcurrant could be used.

6 oz plain flour (175 g)

3 oz ground hazelnuts (75 g)

2 oz icing sugar, sifted (50 g)

The finely grated rind of 1 lemon

¼ teaspoon cinnamon

Freshly grated nutmeg
4 oz butter (110 g)
2 egg yolks
12 oz cranberry jelly (350 g)
2 teaspoons lemon juice
A little icing sugar

Pre-heat the oven to gas mark 5, 375°F (190°C)

A 9 inch (23 cm) round, fluted flan tin with a removable base, well buttered

First combine the flour, ground hazelnuts, icing sugar, lemon rind, cinnamon and a few gratings of whole nutmeg in a bowl, then rub in the butter until the mixture is crumbly. Stir in the egg yolks and form the mixture into a dough. Weigh a 5 oz (150 g) piece of the pastry dough and put it on one side. Roll out the rest on a floured surface to a 10 inch (25·5 cm) round. Place this in the base of the tin and, using your fingers, gradually ease the dough up the side of the tin so that it stands up above the edge. Smooth the base out with your hands.

Next, mix the jelly with the lemon juice and spoon all but 2 tablespoons onto the pastry, smoothing it out evenly to the edge. Use the rest of the dough to make a lattice-work pattern on the top, with strips about $\frac{1}{3}$ inch ($\frac{1}{2}$–1 cm) wide. Then go round the pastry edge with a fork, turning it over inside the edge of the tin to give about a $\frac{1}{2}$ inch (1 cm) border all round.

Bake on a high shelf for 30 minutes, or until the pastry is golden brown. Then, as soon as the flan comes out of the oven, use the reserved jam to fill up the squares formed by the lattice. Sift icing sugar over the top and serve it warm or cold with whipped cream.

Rich fruit cakes

My recipe is the one I always make for a 'celebration' cake. It is more or less my mother's recipe and I have made it for Christmas, birthdays and weddings. It is very rich and if you prefer a fruit cake with a lighter, crumblier texture I recommend the *Traditional Dundee cake* in Part Two, page 276.

Rich fruit cakes are best made about eight weeks before they are needed, but if you can't manage this, it's not a disaster: they just *taste* better if they mature a little.

The recipe which follows is for an 8 inch (20 cm) round cake or a 7 inch (18 cm) square one—just the right size for Christmas and I have given the directions for a simple and *quick* decoration using almond paste and royal icing.

Rich fruit cake

1 lb currants (450 g)
6 oz sultanas (175 g)
6 oz raisins (175 g)
2 oz glacé cherries, rinsed and finely chopped (50 g)
2 oz mixed peel, finely chopped (50 g)
3 tablespoons brandy

8 oz plain flour (225 g)
½ teaspoon salt
¼ teaspoon freshly grated nutmeg
½ teaspoon mixed spice
2 oz almonds, chopped (50 g)—the skins can be left on
8 oz soft brown sugar (225 g)
1 dessertspoon black treacle
8 oz unsalted butter (225 g)
4 eggs
The grated rind of 1 lemon
The grated rind of 1 orange

Pre-heat the oven to gas mark 1, 275°F (140°C)

An 8 inch (20 cm) round cake tin, or a 7 inch (18 cm) square tin, greased and lined with greaseproof paper

The night before you make the cake, place all the dried fruit and peel in a bowl and mix in the brandy. Cover the bowl with a cloth and leave to soak for at least 12 hours.

It is quite a good idea before you measure the treacle to place the tin in the warming drawer of the oven, so that it melts a little.

Sieve the flour, salt and spices into a large mixing bowl, and in a separate bowl cream the butter and sugar together until the mixture's light and fluffy (this in fact is the most important part of the cake, so don't cut any corners). Next beat up the eggs and —a tablespoonful at a time—add them to the creamed mixture, beating thoroughly after each addition. If it looks as if it might start to curdle, you can prevent this happening by adding a little of the flour.

When all the egg has been added, fold in the flour and spices (fold, don't beat). Now stir in the fruit and peel that has been soaking, the nuts, the treacle and the grated lemon and orange rinds.

Spoon the mixture into the prepared cake tin, and spread it out evenly with the back of a spoon. (If you are not going to ice the cake, at this stage you can arrange some whole blanched almonds over the surface—but do it lightly, or else they disappear for ever into the cake!)

Tie a band of brown paper around the outside of the tin, and cover the top of the cake with a double square of greaseproof paper (with a hole in the middle approximately the size of a 50p). Bake the cake on the lower shelf of the oven for $4\frac{1}{2}$–$4\frac{3}{4}$ hours, and don't open the door to peek at it until at least 4 hours have passed. When the cake is cold, wrap it well in double greaseproof paper and store in an airtight tin. I like to 'feed' it at odd intervals with brandy during the storage time. To do this, strip off the lining papers, make a few extra holes in the top with a thin darning needle and pour a few teaspoonfuls of brandy in to soak into the cake. Repeat this at intervals of a week or two.

Christmas cake

For a basic and uncomplicated icing, I've chosen a layer of almond paste topped with a semi-rough royal icing, decorated with almond paste flowers (in this case poinsettias). Ideally the cake should be almond iced at least seven days before the royal icing is put on—to give it a chance to dry out. Otherwise the almond oil may seep through and discolour the royal icing. The thick 'snowy' icing in this recipe, however, should keep the oil at bay even if you (like me) find that sometimes you still have the cake decorating to do on Christmas Eve!

An 8 inch (20 cm) round cake or a 7 inch (18 cm) square cake, made from the rich fruit cake recipe, page 504

For the almond paste: *

1 lb ground almonds (450 g)

8 oz caster sugar (225 g)

8 oz icing sugar (225 g)

2 eggs

2 egg yolks—reserve the whites for the royal icing (see below)

½ teaspoon almond essence

1 teaspoon brandy

1 teaspoon lemon juice

Red, green and yellow food colouring

* Part of this is used to ice the cake, the rest is used to model the flower decorations

For the royal icing:

4 egg whites—combine three but keep one separate

Approximately 1 lb 2 oz sifted icing sugar (500 g)

1 teaspoon glycerine

To make the almond paste, begin by sieving the two sugars into a large bowl and stirring in the eggs and egg yolks. Put the bowl over a pan of barely simmering water and whisk for about 12 minutes until the mixture is thick and fluffy. Then remove the bowl from the heat and sit the base in a couple of inches of cold water.

Next whisk in the essence, brandy and lemon juice and carry on whisking until the mixture is cool. Stir in the ground almonds and knead to form a firm paste. Weigh out 6 oz (175 g) of the paste and reserve this (in a bowl covered with clingfilm) for making the flower decoration.

Divide the rest of the paste in half and roll out one piece into a shape approximately 1 inch (2·5 cm) larger than the top of the cake (your working surface should be kept dusted with some sifted icing sugar so that the paste doesn't stick to it). Brush the top of the cake with egg white, then invert the cake to sit centrally on the almond paste and then with a palette knife press the paste up around the edge of the cake. Now turn the cake the right way up and brush the sides with egg white.

Roll out the other half of the paste into a rectangle and trim it so that it measures half the circumference of the cake by twice the height of the cake (use a piece of string to measure this). Now cut the paste rectangle in half lengthwise, and lightly press the two strips onto the sides of the cake. Smooth over the joins with a knife, and leave the cake covered with a cloth to dry out.

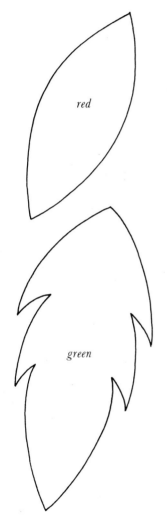

red

green

To make the almond paste poinsettias, take out the paste reserved for decoration. Now using a skewer (so as not to overdo it) colour a small piece about the size of a walnut, yellow. Divide the remaining paste in half, colouring one half of it green, the other red. Using the drawings on the left as a guide, cut out templates in stiff paper or card. Roll out both colours of paste to about $\frac{1}{8}$ inch (3 mm) thick, then with the aid of the templates cut out 6 red leaves and 6 green. Trace a suggestion of veins on the surface with the back of the knife. Leave the leaves to dry, face upwards over a rolling pin. Model the yellow paste into some small pea-sized balls and leave everything to dry overnight.

To make the royal icing, place the three egg whites in a grease-free bowl. Then stir in the icing sugar, a spoonful at a time, until the icing falls thickly from the spoon. At that point, stop adding any more sugar and whisk with an electric mixer for 10 minutes or until the icing stands up in stiff peaks, then stir in the glycerine. Now spoon half the icing into a screw-top jar and put aside in the fridge. Beat about 2 teaspoons more egg white into the remaining half of the icing.

Next use a dab of icing to fix the cake to a 10 inch (25·5 cm) cakeboard, then spread about two-thirds of the remainder on top of the cake. Work the icing back and forth to get rid of any tiny air bubbles, then take a clean plastic ruler and holding it at each end, glide it once over the surface of the cake to give a smooth finish.

Hold the ruler vertically and remove any surplus icing from the top edges of the cake, then spread the remaining icing onto the sides of the cake. Keeping your ruler vertical, turn the cake round in one sweep to smooth the sides—a turntable is ideal for this, but two plates set base to base will also do the job. Now leave the cake for 24 hours for the icing to dry.

To finish off: mark the centre of the cake with a $3\frac{1}{4}$ inch (8 cm) plain circular cutter, then taking your reserved icing from the screw-top jar, spread it thickly outside the marked circle. Use a broad-bladed knife to 'spike' the icing into snow-like peaks. At the edges, bring the peaks over and down to give the effect of hanging snowy icicles (see the drawing below). Lastly lay the green almond paste leaves in the centre of the cake, then the red leaves on top of them. Place the small yellow 'berries' in the centre, fixing them in place with a little icing. Set the whole effect off with a red ribbon, tied in a bow around the cake.

Quantities and cooking times for other sizes of cake

The size of your cake will obviously depend on the number of people you need to cater for. You may need more than one tier for a very special occasion such as a wedding. As a guide, I estimate that the 8 inch (20 cm) cake on page 504 would be sufficient for between 25 and 40 people. The easiest way for me to give you the ingredients and cooking times for the different sizes of cake is in a chart. The method in all cases is the same as that on pages 504–505.

	6 inch (15 cm)	9 inch (23 cm)	11 inch (28 cm)
Currants	8 oz (225 g)	1 lb 4 oz (560 g)	2 lb (900 g)
Sultanas	3 oz (75 g)	8 oz (225 g)	12 oz (350 g)
Raisins	3 oz (75 g)	8 oz (225 g)	12 oz (350 g)
Glacé cherries, rinsed and finely chopped	1½ oz (40 g)	2½ oz (60 g)	4 oz (110 g)
Mixed peel, finely chopped	1½ oz (40 g)	2½ oz (60 g)	4 oz (110 g)
Brandy	3 tablespoons	4 tablespoons	6 tablespoons
Plain flour	4 oz (110 g)	10 oz (275 g)	1 lb (450 g)
Salt	Pinch	½ teaspoon	½ teaspoon
Freshly-grated nutmeg	¼ teaspoon	½ teaspoon	½ teaspoon
Mixed spice	¼ teaspoon	¾ teaspoon	1 teaspoon
Almonds, chopped	1½ oz (40 g)	2½ oz (60 g)	4 oz (110 g)
Soft brown sugar	4 oz (110 g)	10 oz (275 g)	1 lb (450 g)
Black treacle	1 teaspoon (rounded)	1 tablespoon	2 dessertspoons
Unsalted butter	4 oz (110 g)	10 oz (275 g)	1 lb (450 g)
Eggs	2	5	8
Grated lemon rind	½ lemon	1 large lemon	2 lemons
Grated orange rind	½ orange	1 large orange	2 oranges
Cooking times (approximate)	3½ hours	4¾ hours	5½ hours

Almond paste for different sizes of cake

The ingredients below differ slightly from my quick almond paste on page 506, and to fix this paste to the cake I use apricot jam instead of egg white. In this case, I think it is essential to let the almond-iced cake dry for at least a week before applying any royal icing, especially if the iced cake is going to be kept a while before being eaten. If you are going to ice it and eat it very soon afterwards, 2 days drying will be enough.

	6 inch (15 cm)	9 inch (23 cm)	11 inch (28 cm)
Ground almonds	8 oz (225 g)	1 lb (450 g)	1 lb 8 oz (675 g)
Icing sugar, sifted	4 oz (110 g)	8 oz (225 g)	12 oz (350 g)
Caster sugar	4 oz (110 g)	8 oz (225 g)	12 oz (350 g)
Almond essence	2 drops	½ teaspoon	1 teaspoon
Lemon juice	½ teaspoon	1 teaspoon	2 teaspoons
Sherry	1 dessertspoon	1–2 tablespoons	2–3 tablespoons
Egg yolks	3	5	8
Apricot jam (warmed)			

Mix all the dry ingredients together first, then stir in the almond essence, sherry, lemon juice and egg yolks and combine everything to form a stiff paste. Transfer the paste to a pastryboard (dusted with icing sugar) and knead it into a ball. Try not to handle it *too* much—the heat of your hands might make it oily. Warm the apricot jam and brush it over the top and sides of the cake. Now take about half the paste and roll it out to a shape approximately 1 inch (2·5 cm) larger than the top of the cake. Then invert the cake onto the paste shape and trim around the edges if you need to.

Next roll out the rest of the paste into an oblong which is half the circumference and twice the height of the cake (use some string or a tape measure to get these measurements), then cut the oblong in half lengthwise. Roll up one strip. Lightly place one end against the side of the cake and unroll the paste, pressing firmly to the cake as you go. Repeat with the other strip to complete the sides of the cake and press the joins together. Turn the cake the right way up, even the surfaces with a rolling pin and store in a double sheet of greaseproof paper for at least a week before applying royal icing.

Royal icing for different sizes of cake

If your cake is in tiers then, in order to support the weight of one tier on top of another, you are going to need *three* layers of this hard-set icing. If it has only one tier, then a single thick layer with the quantities below will be all right (you can also add 2–3 teaspoons of glycerine to give a softer texture, if preferred). The cake boards for a tiered cake in each case need to be 2–3 inches wider than the width of the cake itself. Useful items of equipment would be a turntable, palette knife and plastic icing scraper.

	6 inch (15 cm)	9 inch (23 cm)	11 inch (28 cm)
Icing sugar	1 lb (450 g)	1½ lb (700 g)	2 lb (900 g)
Egg whites	2–3	4	6

Place the egg whites in your largest bowl (and make sure it is grease-free), then stir in the sifted icing sugar, two spoonfuls at a time. When it is all stirred in, take an electric mixer and whisk at top speed for about 10 minutes, by which time the icing should be standing up in peaks at least 2 inches (5 cm) high. As soon as you reach this stage, cover the bowl with a damp cloth to prevent the icing drying out.

Use a little icing to stick the cake to the board, then place the board on the turntable and give the cake one coat of icing—using one-third of the quantity. Ice the top of the cake first, and then the sides with the aid of a palette knife. Get the sides smooth with a plastic scraper, and the top with a palette knife dipped into hot water and shaken. Smooth the icing right up to the edge of the board too. Store the rest of the icing in a plastic container, and leave the cake to dry overnight. Then give it the second and third coats, leaving each coat to dry overnight.

Decoration
Even for a special occasion cake, I find the simpler the design the better, keeping piping to an absolute minimum and using roses made from modelling paste. These roses can be tinted in various colours and offset by gold or silver paper leaves. Finish off with satin ribbon tied around the cake or around each tier.

Modelling paste

2 oz lard (50 g)
2 tablespoons lemon juice
1½ lb sifted icing sugar (700 g)
Food colouring (according to your design)

Heat the lard and lemon juice with 2 tablespoons of water until the fat melts. Then stir in ½ lb (225 g) of the icing sugar, and cook over a very low heat until the sugar dissolves and turns a semi-opaque colour (about 2 minutes). Then remove the pan from the heat and stir in the rest of the sugar which will eventually give you a mixture the consistency of dough.

Turn it out onto a working surface dusted with sugar, knead for a few seconds, then divide it in half and work in whatever colours you have chosen. Add the colour with a skewer in *small* drops until you arrive at the right shade. The paste should be stored in a

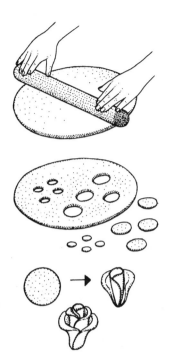

plastic bag, and when you're ready, roll out the paste and cut out some small, circular shapes the size of a 10p piece, and some slightly smaller than 5p pieces. Make up the roses as in the drawings on the left, curving the circular pieces around and pinching them gently into shape. Leave them to dry on a tray overnight.

Arrange the roses how you like, with some gold or silver paper leaves here and there, sticking them on to the cake with small amounts of icing. To neaten the edges of the cake at the base and top, you could pipe a tiny row of beads (using an icing bag fitted with a large, plain no. 1 nozzle). Finally tie bands of ribbon in place around the cake or around each of the tiers.

Pâtés and starters

Including recipes for:

The whole idea of a first course (or starter, as it's become more popularly known) is that it should encourage the appetite, rather than spoil it. There's nothing worse than having to first struggle through a huge slab of rich pâté (and the bread needed to get it down), and then have to cope with a main course! In fact my enjoyment of special occasions at multi-starred restaurants has often been marred, simply because I couldn't find a plain enough starter to really appreciate the skills lavished on the main course. For me the biggest problem comes when I am confronted with an hors-d'oeuvre trolley.

Hors-d'oeuvre means literally 'outside work', which reflects the attitude of most 19th century French chefs, who preferred to sub-contract the tedious job of preparing it. Most countries have some kind of hors-d'oeuvre: the Scandinavians their smørrebrød, the Italians their antipasti, the Spaniards their entremeses; but it was in France the hors-d'oeuvre reached truly epic proportions —and also in Russia, where a separate room was often set aside for it! We still find the legacy of this in some restaurants, where an awesome array of meats, fish dishes, salads, eggs, canapés and so on get trundled in while glazed looks come over the faces of the diners. It is very tempting to load the plate with a selection of everything, and finish up with a complete meal rather than a starter. That, of course, destroys the whole point of a first course, so perhaps it's just as well it isn't very practical for us to go to such lengths at home.

Now I accept that not everybody will share my simple tastes in food, but I still think it is a safe general rule to have only one rich course in a meal. (In fact I have deliberately made a distinction between pâtés and starters in the title of this chapter because I prefer, on the whole, to serve pâtés on their own for lunch or supper, with plenty of crusty bread, and some pickled gherkins and a side-salad to counteract the richness.)

My own favourite starters tend to need little or no cooking: a *Tomato salad* (served in late summer when the tomatoes are red and ripe), with fresh basil, parsley, a little chopped shallot and some good vinaigrette is almost unbeatable. Some thinly sliced *Parma ham*, or salami or mortadella (or a mixture of all three), served with preserved pimentoes and French bread spread with unsalted Normandy butter, would also be a real treat. I think it is the salady starters that seem to sharpen the appetite best. *Avocado vinaigrette* is a popular one, but *Asparagus* or *Artichoke vinaigrette* come into the same category. Other firm favourites in our house are *Egg mayonnaise* and *Eggs en cocotte* but since they are slightly richer than some other starters, one must take care to serve a portion that won't spoil the main course.

Before giving some recipes for first courses, and a number of pâtés, let me offer some suggestions for starters that are simple to prepare and make no strenuous demands on the appetite.

Charcuterie

This is the name given to a whole range of cooked, dried, salted or smoked meats, which can be served either separately or mixed.

Prosciutto (Parma ham) This is the Italian raw cured ham, which is cut into almost transparently thin slices. It is often served with slices of melon, but I must say I prefer it by itself or mixed with other meats.

Salami (salted matured sausage) This comes in many nationalities, Danish, French, German—but for me the best of all is the Italian. If you are fortunate enough to be offered a choice, ask for *Casalinga* which is usually one of the rougher, country varieties.

Mortadella (large smooth boiled pork sausage) Real Italian mortadella is normally 12–18 inches (30–45 cm) in diameter (the smaller kind is not Italian and never as good). It looks like spam; but don't be deceived: its mildly spicy flavour is something quite different.

Mixed together, 4 oz (110 g) of each of the above will serve 6 people as a first course. As an accompaniment I would suggest some preserved pimentoes (bright red and yellow peppers which are sold in jars), black olives, and some Italian mixed pickles, which are usually a selection of preserved carrots, baby onions, cauliflower and celery.

Other forms of charcuterie also make very suitable first course dishes. In the end it's a matter of finding out where they are sold—in Britain usually in delicatessens or specialised food stores—and making your own choice.

Cheese for starters

Cheese is traditionally eaten at the end of a meal in this country, but there are at least two cheeses that make excellent first courses, served as they would be in their country of origin:

Mozzarella fresca (fresh Mozzarella) Originally made from buffalo milk (but now often from cow's milk), this soft white cheese is to be seen in some shops in little plastic bags steeping in a bowl of cold water, which is the way it should also be stored at home in the refrigerator. Serve it cut into slices, with some sliced tomatoes, rock salt and coarsely ground pepper, and a drizzle of olive oil poured over.

Feta This crumbly, creamy-tasting cheese is the basis of a *Greek salad*. The recipe for this delicious salad is given in the section on cheese in Part Two, pages 475–476. It will serve 4 people as a first course.

Crudités

This is the generic title for various arrangements of raw vegetables or salad ingredients, served with a sauce such as *Aioli sauce* (see page 578) or *Avocado sauce* (Part One, page 160). The different vegetables are often cut into long strips, dipped into the sauce, and then eaten with the fingers. An alternative—and perhaps better arrangement— is to shred or grate the ingredients. Grated carrot, shredded raw cabbage, thin slivers of raw fennel, some slices of cucumber, and thin strips of red or green pepper would make an attractive combination. Prepare each ingredient in separate bowls and sprinkle over a little (not too much) vinaigrette. Then arrange a selection of the vegetables in a pretty pattern on each plate, spooning a dollop of *Aioli sauce* or *Avocado sauce* in the centre.

Asparagus or artichoke

In their season these make excellent starters. Details for cooking and serving both of them are included in the Vegetable chapter (pages 635–656).

Fish

Most varieties of smoked fish and shellfish can be served as starters; recipes and suggestions for these can be found in the relevant chapter in Part Two, pages 439–460. Other fish that might be considered are:

Sardines Portuguese are the best and are delicious served with nothing more than a little tomato salad and some crusty bread. Or as a variation you might try the following:

Sardine-stuffed tomatoes
For 4–6 people, mash up the contents of two tins of sardines (oil as well), then add to this 3 inches (7·5 cm) of cucumber finely

chopped, half a green pepper finely chopped, 2 tablespoons of mayonnaise, 1 clove of garlic crushed, a generous pinch of cayenne and 2 tablespoons of lemon juice. Season the mixture well, then pack it into 8 small or 6 largish hollowed-out and well-drained tomatoes. Serve with some wholewheat bread and butter.

Pickled Herrings (Rollmops) These can be bought in jars from any supermarket, and I always find it best to rinse them under a cold tap then pat them dry with kitchen paper, in case they are too vinegary. Serve them with sliced pickled dill cucumber, chopped beetroot and soured cream. A similarly interesting first course would be:

Russian herring
Place a slice of buttered rye bread on four small plates, and on top of each slice arrange one pickled herring folded into three. Top this with some thinly sliced onion rings, followed by a whole slice of apple (Cox's are good). Finally cover with a dollop of soured cream—5 fl oz (150 ml) for four people—and scatter some fresh snipped chives all over.

Tuna This is very useful. It can be flaked over a *Salad Niçoise* (page 594), which can be served as a first course provided the portions are not too large; or it goes particularly well with white beans—see the recipe on page 522.

Anchovies These are always a good standby in the larder, but especially for making first courses. They can be used as a simple hors-d'oeuvre accompanied by a few salad ingredients, or if you want to make *Egg mayonnaise* with bought mayonnaise (salad cream just *won't* do) a few strips of anchovy as a garnish will perk it up a lot.

Melon
There are several types of melon which, if they are bought in good condition, can make a very nice start to a meal. My complaint is that in some restaurants the melon is often served over-chilled—or worse still, it has been kept uncovered in the refrigerator and has absorbed other flavours! So always store melons in sealed polythene bags, and remember to bring them out of the fridge in time to reach room temperature.

To test melons for ripeness, press the opposite end of the fruit from the stalk with your thumb—if it gives a bit, then the fruit is ripe. A ripe melon should smell fragrant too.

Although sugar and ginger are traditional accompaniments, in my opinion a good melon doesn't need anything at all to go with it. I once had a beautiful Cantaloupe melon ruined by being drowned in port (all I could taste in the end was the port). However a good summery starter would be a mixture of chopped melon and some halved, de-pipped grapes sprinkled with lots of fresh chopped mint and a dressing (made with one part cider vinegar to four parts oil). Served in glass goblets it does look most attractive.

The most popular varieties of melon are:

Cantaloupe (Musk melon) These are usually small and green, with a very rough skin. Inside the flesh is deep orange with a lovely perfumed flavour.

Charentais These too are small melons, with a yellow-green skin and a golden yellow flesh with a distinctive flavour.

Ogen This is another small melon, easily distinguished by its yellow and green striped skin. Inside the flesh is green.

Honeydew These are larger and more commonly available than the others. Sometimes they sport a dark green skin, sometimes a bright yellow one. The flavour depends on their ripeness: a really ripe one will be juicy and fragrant, an under-ripe one watery and tasteless.

Fresh fruit and mint vinaigrette

(serves 6 people)

This is an unusual first course which really sharpens the appetite. I like to serve it in tall, stemmed glasses which makes it look pretty and appealing.

2 dessert apples, cored and diced but with skins left on
2 medium-sized pears, cored and diced but unpeeled
The juice of half a lemon
2 oranges, peeled and cut into chunks
4 oz grapes, halved and de-pipped (110 g)
1 tablespoon fresh chopped mint
For the dressing:
3 tablespoons wine vinegar
6 tablespoons olive oil

1 level teaspoon salt
4 tablespoons double cream

To garnish:
6 sprigs fresh mint

Dice the apples and pears straight into a bowl, and pour the lemon juice over them to prevent discolouring. Stir gently to coat all the pieces, then add the grapes and orange chunks, stir in the chopped mint, cover the bowl with cling film and chill in the fridge for a couple of hours.

To make the dressing, place the salt and wine vinegar in a bowl, leave for a few minutes for the salt to dissolve, then add the olive oil. Whisk well to blend, then stir in the double cream.

When you're ready to serve, divide the fruit between six glasses, pour the dressing over and garnish each with a sprig of fresh mint.

Avocado vinaigrette

(serves 6 people)

This is one of my own favourite first courses, if the avocados are buttery soft and the vinaigrette is well made.

3 ripe avocados
1 quantity of vinaigrette dressing (see page 576), using a large clove of garlic
6 crisp lettuce leaves
1 tablespoon fresh snipped chives

Ideally the avocados shouldn't be halved until just before serving, but if you're at all anxious as to whether they're sound or not then you can halve them and have a look about an hour before serving—but *don't* remove the stone. If they look sound, then just replace the halves together and wrap in clingfilm. Serve each half sitting on a lettuce leaf (if it won't sit straight, make a depression on the underside with your thumb, and this might help).

To serve, split the avocados in half and remove the stones. If at all possible, don't do this until *just* before serving because they do tend to discolour quickly. Serve each half on a crisp lettuce leaf, spoon some of the vinaigrette into the hollows left by the stone and sprinkle with the chives. Have some extra dressing on the table along with some crusty bread and creamy butter.

Avocado mousse with prawns and vinaigrette

(serves 8 people)

This is a delicious, creamy and most attractive starter for a dinner party. But don't make it too far in advance as it tends to lose its beautiful colour.

2 ripe avocados
½ oz powdered gelatine (10 g)
5 fl oz hot chicken stock (150 ml)
The juice of half a lemon
1 clove garlic, finely chopped
5 fl oz double cream, lightly whipped (150 ml)
5 fl oz mayonnaise—see page 577 (150 ml)
3 oz peeled prawns (75 g)
Salt and freshly-milled black pepper
1 quantity vinaigrette dressing (page 576)

8 small ramekins, lightly oiled

Put 3 tablespoons of the stock and the gelatine in a bowl and stand it in a pan of simmering water. Stir until the gelatine is dissolved, then pour into the goblet of a liquidiser with the rest of the stock. Next skin and stone the avocados, chop the flesh roughly and add it to the liquidiser (include the darker green part that clings to the skin—this will help the colour). Now add the lemon juice and garlic, and blend until it's completely smooth.

Empty the mixture into a bowl and stir in the whipped cream and the mayonnaise very thoroughly, then season with salt and pepper. Spoon the mixture into the lightly-oiled ramekins, cover them with cling film and pop them into the fridge to set.

When you're ready to serve, slide a palette knife around the edge of each ramekin and ease the mousse away from the sides. Turn the mousses out onto serving plates, top each one of them with some of the prawns, and sprinkle some vinaigrette over each serving. Have plenty of crusty bread ready to go with this.

Avocado and seafood salad

(serves 4 people)

A distinct improvement on the inevitable prawn cocktail as a starter.

4 oz peeled prawns or fresh crabmeat (110 g)
2 ripe avocados

1 quantity of yoghurt seafood sauce (see page 570)
A few crisp lettuce leaves, shredded

For the garnish
Cayenne pepper
4 lemon wedges
4 sprigs watercress or some chopped parsley

First halve and peel the avocados, removing the stones, then chop the flesh into small ($\frac{1}{2}$ inch, 1 cm) pieces. Now arrange some shredded lettuce in 4 stemmed glasses or bowls, and divide the chopped avocados equally between each one. Next sprinkle the prawns—equally—over the avocado, then spoon the sauce over. Serve each one with a wedge of lemon to squeeze over, a faint dusting of cayenne pepper, and a sprig of watercress or some chopped parsley as a garnish.

Marinaded mushrooms

(serves 4 people)

These have a really delicious flavour and can be made well ahead.

8 oz dark-gilled mushrooms, wiped and sliced (225 g)
6 rashers streaky bacon, chopped small
2 cloves of garlic, very finely chopped
4 tablespoons olive oil
8 fl oz red wine (225 ml)
2 tablespoons fresh chopped parsley
6 lettuce leaves
Salt and freshly-milled black pepper

Heat the olive oil in a large frying pan, then add the chopped bacon and fry until the fat begins to run. Then add the sliced mushrooms, along with the garlic and cook for another couple of minutes—shaking the pan and stirring the mushrooms around all the time. Now pour in the red wine, turn the heat up high and let it all bubble for a minute or two and reduce a little.

Turn the heat down and cook for a further 4 minutes. Season to taste and transfer to a serving dish. Allow the mushrooms to cool before popping the dish into the refrigerator to chill. Serve on crisp lettuce leaves with some fresh chopped parsley sprinkled on top.

Fresh tomato soup with basil

(serves 4 people)

1½ lb red, ripe tomatoes (700 g), cut in quarters (leave the skins on)
1 medium-sized onion, chopped small
1 medium-sized potato, chopped small
1 clove garlic, crushed
½ pint stock (275 ml)
2 teaspoons fresh, chopped basil
1½ tablespoons olive oil (preferably good quality)
Salt and freshly-milled black pepper

Gently heat up the olive oil in a thick saucepan, then put in the onion and potato and let them soften slowly without browning. This takes 10–15 minutes.

Now add the tomatoes, stir well and let them cook for a minute. Pour the stock over the tomatoes, stir, season with salt and pepper and add the garlic. Cover and allow to simmer for 25 minutes.

When the soup is ready, pass the whole lot through a sieve to extract the skins and pips. Taste to check the seasoning, add the basil, then re-heat and serve with crusty French bread. If the weather is hot, this soup is just as delicious served ice-cold.

Note: if you cannot get fresh basil use 1 teaspoon of dried, adding it at the same time as the tomatoes.

White bean and tuna fish salad

(serves 6 people)

This Italian dish (otherwise known as *Tonno e fagioli*) is one of my husband's favourite first courses—so I have to include it here!

8 oz haricot beans (long variety) (225 g)
1 onion, cut in half
1 carrot, cut into chunks
1 bayleaf
1 sprig of thyme
1 × 7 oz tin tuna fish in oil (200 g)
1 Spanish onion, sliced thinly and separated into rings
2 level tablespoons chopped parsley
Salt and freshly-milled black pepper
Crisp lettuce leaves for serving

For the dressing:
1 tablespoon lemon juice
1 teaspoon wine vinegar
1 teaspoon dried mustard powder
1 teaspoon salt
Freshly-milled black pepper
2 cloves garlic, crushed
5 tablespoons olive oil

The beans should be soaked overnight, or else covered with plenty of cold water, brought to the boil, simmered for 5 minutes, then left to soak for two hours. After that add the onion halves, carrot, bayleaf and thyme (but don't add any salt) and simmer the beans again for about an hour—or until they're tender.

While they are cooking make the dressing (directions on page 576). Then as soon as the beans are cooked, drain them thoroughly in a colander, removing the onion, carrot and herbs, and tip them into a large salad bowl. Pour the dressing over them while they are still warm (so they can really soak up all the delicious flavours).

Meanwhile drain the tuna fish and break it up into largish flakes. When the beans have cooled, and you're ready to serve, stir in the onion rings, tuna flakes and parsley. Taste and season with salt and pepper as required, then arrange the salad on six individual plates lined with crisp lettuce leaves, and sprinkle a bit more parsley over each serving if you like.

Smoked fish creams

(serves 8 people)

Serve these light, puffy little creams garnished with plenty of watercress and some *Quick Hollandaise* (Part One, page 39) as a sauce. A delicious first course for a special occasion.

10 oz smoked haddock fillets (275 g)
2 eggs, lightly beaten
Whole nutmeg
½ pint double cream (275 ml)
Salt and freshly-milled black pepper

Eight 2½ inch (6 cm) ramekin dishes, well buttered

Begin by carefully skinning the fish (you should have about 8 oz (225 g) of flesh after this). Cut the fish into pieces about 1½ inches (3·5 cm) square and place them in a liquidiser or food processor, along with a little salt, pepper and some freshly grated nutmeg. Switch the machine on and blend until the fish has turned to a smooth, even pulp. Then blend in the lightly beaten eggs. Transfer the mixture to a bowl, cover with clingfilm and leave it in the fridge overnight, or at least for 6 hours.

When you're ready to cook the fish creams, pre-heat the oven to gas mark 5, 375°F (190°C). Fill a large roasting tin with about 1 inch (2·5 cm) of boiling water and put this on the centre shelf of the oven. Next return the fish mixture to the liquidiser together with the cream, and blend them together thoroughly. Fill each ramekin three-quarters full with the mixture, then place all the ramekins in the tin containing the hot water. Cook for exactly 30 minutes. Serve the creams immediately, either in the ramekins or turned out onto plates (do this by holding each ramekin with a cloth, tipping the creams upside down onto the palm of your hand and then straight onto a plate the right way up).

Asparagus and cheese tart

(serves 4–6 people)

Once you start to grow a bed of asparagus, you find you can hardly keep up with the harvesting during the season. But for those who don't grow their own—and have to pay high prices in the market—here is a recipe for a first course that makes a little go a long way.

For the pastry:
4 oz plain flour (110 g)
A pinch of salt
1 oz lard (25 g)
1 oz margarine (25 g)
Cold water, to mix

For the filling:
¾ lb asparagus (350 g), approximately 15 medium-sized stalks
2 large fresh eggs

1½ oz Cheddar cheese, grated (40 g)
1 level tablespoon grated Parmesan cheese
½ pint double cream (275 ml)
Salt and freshly-milled black pepper

Pre-heat the oven to gas mark 4, 350°F (180°C) and pop a baking sheet in to pre-heat as well.

An 8 inch (20 cm) round flan tin, greased

First of all make up the pastry, then roll it out and line a flan tin with it. Prick the base all over with a fork and cook for 10 minutes, then take it out of the oven and turn the heat up to gas mark 5, 375°F (190°C).

The asparagus meanwhile should be half-cooked (five minutes in a steamer), then cut into 1½ inch (4 cm) lengths. Arrange the asparagus evenly over the pastry base, then sprinkle in the Cheddar cheese. Now whisk the eggs until frothy, and beat them into the cream together with a good seasoning of salt and freshly-milled black pepper. Pour this cream mixture over the asparagus and cheese, and sprinkle the Parmesan on top.

Place the tart on the pre-heated baking sheet in the oven for 40–45 minutes, or until the centre is firm and the filling golden-brown and puffy. This tart is delicious eaten hot or cold.

Chicken liver pâté

(serves 4–6 people)

This is a fine smooth velvety pâté, which will serve 4 people for a lunch or 6 people as a first course.

8 oz chicken livers (225 g)
6 oz butter, room temperature (175 g)
2 extra oz butter, for melting (50 g)
2 tablespoons brandy
2 level teaspoons mustard powder
¼ teaspoon powdered mace
1 level teaspoon fresh chopped thyme, or ¼ teaspoon dried thyme
2 cloves garlic, crushed
Salt and freshly-milled black pepper

Take a good thick frying pan, melt about 1 oz (25 g) butter in it, and fry the chicken livers over a medium heat for about 5 minutes. Keep them on the move, turning them over quite frequently. Then remove them from the pan, using a draining spoon and transfer them to an electric blender, or press them through a nylon sieve.

Now melt the rest of the 6 oz (175 g) butter and add this to the blender. Then pour the brandy onto the juices left in the frying pan (this is to rinse it out), and pour that over the liver. Then add the mustard, mace, thyme and garlic, season well with salt and pepper, and blend till you have a smooth purée.

Next press the whole lot into an earthenware pot, or 6 individual pots, pour the 2 oz (50 g) melted butter over, leave it to get quite cold, then cover with foil or clingfilm and leave it in the bottom of the fridge for a day or two. This is nice served with hot toast, sprigs of watercress, some silver-skinned onions and a few gherkins.

Rillettes de Tours (pork pâté)

(serves 6–8 people)

This is famous around the Loire district of France and sold everywhere in charcuteries—sometimes in thick chunks from a large terrine or packed into little pots. I would recommend this for anyone who doesn't like liver pâtés.

2 lb piece lean belly pork (900 g)—ask the butcher to remove rind and bones for you
8 oz back pork fat (225 g)
4 fl oz dry white wine (110 ml)
½ teaspoon powdered mace
10 black peppercorns
10 juniper berries
2 cloves garlic, crushed
1 dessertspoon fresh thyme (or 1 rounded teaspoon dried thyme)
1 heaped teaspoon salt

Pre-heat the oven to gas mark 1, 275°F (140°C)

A 2 pint (1·25 litre) earthenware terrine

With your sharpest knife, cut the pork lengthwise into long strips about 1 inch (2·5 cm) wide, then cut each strip across and across again into smaller strips, and place these in the earthenware terrine. Cut the fat into small pieces too, and mix these in (the excess fat will help to keep the pork properly moist during the cooking). Now add the thyme, mace, salt and garlic along with the peppercorns and juniper berries (both crushed with the back of a tablespoon). Then pour in the wine.

Mix everything around to distribute the flavours, cover the terrine, place it in the centre of the oven and leave it there for 4 hours. After that, taste a piece of the pork and add more salt (and pepper) if necessary. Now empty everything into a large sieve standing over a bowl and let all the fat drip through (press the meat gently to extract the fat). Leave the drained fat to get cold.

Next take a couple of forks, and pull the strips of meat into shreds (sometimes it is pounded instead, but personally I think it's worth persevering with the fork method). Then pack the rillettes lightly into the terrine, and leave to get cold. After that, remove the jelly from the bowl of fat, melt it gently and pour it over the rillettes. Then spread a layer of fat over the top to keep it moist. Keep the rillettes in a cool place or in the lowest part of the refrigerator (covered with foil or clingfilm) till needed. Serve with hot toast, crusty bread or crisp baked croûtons.

Country pâté
(serves 10–12 people)

This is a rough well-seasoned pâté—good for outdoor eating or for lunch with lots of crusty bread, a salad and some 'country' wine.

12 oz lean minced beef (350 g)
10 oz lean bacon, chopped small (275 g)
1 lb fat belly pork, minced (450 g)
8 oz pig's liver, minced (225 g)
1 or 2 cloves garlic, crushed
4 fl oz dry white wine (110 ml)
1 fl oz brandy (25 ml)
15 black peppercorns
10 juniper berries

1 rounded teaspoon salt
¼ teaspoon ground mace

A 2 lb (900 g) loaf tin or terrine

The weights given in the ingredients for the meats is *before* preparing e.g. removing rinds and bones from the pork and bacon, fat from the beef and tubes from the liver. If you give your butcher plenty of notice, he'll probably mince your meats for you. If not, use the medium blade of a mincer or chop them in a food processor.

To make the pâté, place the meats and bacon in a large bowl and mix them all very thoroughly. Add the salt, mace and garlic. Crush the peppercorns and juniper berries on a flat surface using the back of a tablespoon, then add to the meat.

Now pour the wine and brandy over, have another really good mix, then cover the bowl with a cloth and leave it in a cool place for a couple of hours. Before cooking the pâté, pre-heat the oven to gas mark 2, 300°F (150°C). Then pack the mixture into a loaf tin and place that in a meat-roasting tin half-filled with hot water. Bake for about 1¾ hours. By the time it has cooked the pâté will have shrunk quite a bit. Remove it from the oven and allow to cool without draining off any of the juices (because when cold, the surrounding fat will keep the pâté moist).

When the pâté is cold, place a double strip of foil across the top and put a few weights on to press it down for a few hours—this pressing isn't essential but it helps to make the pâté less crumbly when you cut it. Serve with hot toast, crusty bread, or croûtons baked until crisp in the oven.

Offal

Including recipes for:

One of my favourite cookery writers, Margaret Costa, once called a chapter on offal 'awful offal'. Not that offal is awful, she explains, but the *name* sounds awful. I agree with her, but find the various alternatives (like 'spare parts') equally off-putting. In fact the whole subject can be discouraging to some people not just because of its anatomical origins—the word itself is derived from those parts that 'fall off' or are rejected when a carcass is dressed—but because so often the meat has been neither sensitively nor imaginatively cooked. Lumps of semi-boiled watery kidney in a steak-and-kidney pie, or unevenly cut paving-slabs of over-cooked liver, these are the real culprits. In working on, and testing for, this chapter I have actually converted several people to offal who would otherwise never have considered eating it!

Offal really has an important place in our diet. Not only can it supply a generous amount of essential nutrients, but it does so at a very economical price. Being rich and concentrated in flavour means a little goes a long way, and items such as ox kidneys and liver, or pork kidneys, provide relatively cheap and quite delicious meals, as I hope the recipes in this chapter will show. But first let's consider some of the items in question.

Liver

Rich in iron and many vitamins, most nutritionists would have us all eat liver at least once a week. In cooking it there are two important considerations. One is to try to persuade an obliging butcher to slice the liver *thinly* and *evenly* for you. And having achieved that, your next objective is to cook it carefully and, if frying or grilling it, quickly. If you cook it too long, it will be tough and dry.

Calves' liver This is the most expensive and said to be the finest flavoured. Serve it thinly sliced and lightly fried (so that it's still slightly pink) in butter, with some crisp fried bacon to go with it.

Ox liver This is the cheapest, but excellent braised with lots of onion and a thick gravy. With its rather coarser texture it isn't suitable for frying or grilling.

Lambs' liver My own favourite. Properly cooked it can be meltingly tender with a delicious flavour. Where you're unable to buy it thinly sliced, try cutting it up into evenly-sized strips, as in *Liver in yoghurt and juniper sauce* (page 535).

Pigs' liver This is extremely strong-flavoured and, in my opinion, not suitable for grilling, frying, or even casseroling. However, it is just the thing for pâtés and terrines and the recipe for *Faggots and peas* (page 537).

Notes on frying and grilling liver

Always wipe the liver as dry as possible with kitchen paper first. Only calves' and lambs' liver are suitable for grilling or frying.

To fry Lightly dust the pieces with seasoned flour and fry in hot butter or oil over a medium heat. It's important to get a good brown crust on the meat, and then only turn once after 3–4 minutes (or when you can see tiny droplets of blood beginning to form on the uncooked surface). Cook for a further 3–4 minutes.

To grill Brush the liver with oil or butter and give it a minute longer on both sides than for frying.

Kidneys

These too are packed full of nutrients. All types of kidney are excellent for cooking, given the appropriate treatment for the right recipe. One point to remember is that kidneys do not have such a good flavour if stored too long. It's best to cook them really fresh, preferably on the day of purchase. If that's not possible, keep them until the next day but no longer.

Veal kidneys These are very expensive and, outside large cities, not easy to come by. They need gentle cooking and are usually served plain or with a light sauce.

Ox kidney This is an essential ingredient for steak-and-kidney pudding (or pie)—no other type of kidney will give the proper, traditional flavour to these dishes. Ox kidney is cheap and, though it is not recommended for grilling or frying, it is excellent stewed, braised, or especially curried (see page 541). Should you want to grate your own suet, by the way, the fat around an ox kidney is the best for this.

Lambs' kidneys I'm particularly fond of plump, juicy lambs' kidneys which are available through the spring and summer months, when home-grown lamb is in its peak season. Frozen or imported, they are never quite as good, so if you buy these in the winter, they do need a good-flavoured sauce to go with them. If you can, buy lambs' kidneys still encased in their own fat, which seems to keep them fresher. It peels off easily, and if you place the fat in a meat roasting-tin in a low oven, it will render down to a bowlful of the most delicious cooking fat (which will have cost you nothing).

Pork kidneys In the past cooks have tended to subject pork kidneys to various periods of pre-soaking and blanching, to tone down what used to be a rather strong flavour. Nowadays, with more intensive meat production, we're eating blander, younger pork and I think this is the reason why the kidneys are milder, tender and quite delicious. They can therefore be cooked without any special treatment and, if you like their flavour, it may be useful to know that pork kidneys can be sliced and used as an alternative in any of the lambs' kidney recipes in this chapter.

Preparation of kidneys

To prepare lambs' or pork kidneys, first remove the skins, then slice the kidneys in half lengthwise. Now use a pair of kitchen scissors to snip out the cores (which look like solid fatty lumps)—simply pinch the cores between your fingers and snip all around them with the scissors. With ox or calves' kidneys the process is just reversed: instead of cutting the core away from the kidney, you snip the lobes of kidney away from the core. (If I'm making a steak-and-kidney pudding, I sometimes pop the cores plus any little pieces of kidney still attached into a pan with an onion, carrot and herbs and boil up some stock, which after skimming makes a delicious gravy for serving with the pudding.)

Tongue

Ox tongue Salting improves the flavour of an ox tongue and so (especially around Christmas or party-time when there's a house full of people to feed) a salted tongue is the best kind to buy. Cooked and pressed and served cold, it goes well with *Cumberland sauce* (Part One, page 156) or *Spiced plum chutney* (page 661). For its preparation and cooking details see page 544.

Lambs' tongues These are nicest braised until the skins slip off easily (which is done by slitting the underside of each tongue and then carefully peeling away the skin), then sliced, re-heated gently and served with a hot *Parsley Sauce* (Part One, page 150) or in a casserole (see page 547).

Oxtail

There is something about the flavour and aroma of an oxtail braising in the oven that's very comforting on a bitter cold winter's day. Choose an oxtail that clearly has plenty of flesh around the bone: one complete oxtail will serve 3–4 people. The recipe on page 548 is particularly good with haricot beans, which seem to absorb so much of the flavour.

Heart
Invariably when I attempt to write about cooking heart, I find the description and detail end up sounding comical. Facts like 'a heart is heavy in proportion to its size' or 'long slow cooking makes a heart tender' almost seem like something out of a romantic novel! Anyway lambs' hearts, in my opinion, are the nicest. Allow one per person, wash in cold water, then use a pair of kitchen scissors to cut out all the tubes and the dividing wall in the centre. You then have a convenient cavity for a stuffing (which I think is really essential).

Sweetbreads
I am often asked what exactly *are* sweetbreads? In fact they're glands, more specifically the thymus and pancreas glands of the animal. They are—rightly—considered to be a great delicacy and are not readily available without pre-ordering. Ox sweetbreads are fairly tough and they need long, slow cooking; calves' sweetbreads are rarer and much more tender; but best of all are lambs' sweetbreads. For the last two the preparation is the same. Pre-soak the sweetbreads in cold water for 1–2 hours; then boil in fresh water: 5 minutes for lambs', 10 minutes for calves'. Cool them in a colander under cold running water then, using a sharp knife, remove any gristle, skin and veins.

Tripe
Tripe is the stomach of an ox. It has to be treated by blanching and pre-soaking, and this is done by the supplier or the butcher. It's this initial treatment that gives tripe its bleached white appearance. Honeycomb tripe—which a friend of mine describes as having the feel and texture of slithery knitting!—is very good when cooked with love and, judging by its regular appearance in supermarkets, is still popular. Normally it needs about an hour's further cooking at home, but this can vary so check cooking times with your supplier. If it is over-done it becomes limp, when ideally it should still have some 'bite' to it.

Peppered liver
(serves 2 people)

This is more or less the same as *Steak au poivre* but quite a bit cheaper and—if you like liver—every bit as good.

12 oz lambs' liver (350 g) —ask the butcher to cut it into the thinnest slices possible
2 teaspoons whole black peppercorns
1 tablespoon flour
1 tablespoon olive oil
1 teaspoon butter
5 fl oz red (or white) wine (150 ml)
1 level teaspoon salt

You'll need to crush the peppercorns first, and this can present one or two problems. If you've got a pestle and mortar you're home and dry; if you haven't, then the best way to crush them is by exerting a lot of pressure on the back of a tablespoon with the peppercorns underneath it. This last method can often result in one or two peppercorns escaping and rolling off onto the floor, if you're not careful. So be warned.

When you've got the peppercorns coarsely crushed, add them to the flour with a level teaspoon of salt. Then dip the pieces of liver in it, pressing the pepper in a bit on both sides. Now in a large heavy-based frying pan, heat the oil and butter to the foamy stage, then put the liver slices in and cook them gently for a minute or two. As soon as the blood starts to run, turn them over, and gently cook them on the other side for slightly less time.

Whatever you do, don't overcook the liver or it will be dry and tough. Transfer the slices onto a warm serving dish, add the wine to the pan, let it bubble and reduce, then pour it over the liver and serve immediately.

Paprika liver
(serves 3–4 people)

This is one of my favourite recipes for liver—quick, simple and quite delicious.

1 lb lambs' liver (450 g), cut into narrow strips about 2½ inches (6 cm) long
1 large onion, very finely chopped
1 green pepper, de-seeded and cut into narrow strips about 1½ inches (4 cm) long

| 5 fl oz soured cream (150 ml) |
| 3 oz butter (75 g) |
| 5 fl oz red wine (150 ml) |
| 1 level tablespoon Hungarian paprika |
| Salt and freshly-milled black pepper |

First melt 2 oz (50 g) of the butter in your largest frying pan, add the onion and green pepper and soften them over a gentle heat for about 7 or 8 minutes. Then transfer the vegetables to a plate using a draining spoon. Now with the heat fairly high, melt the extra butter and add the slices of liver. Let them cook and brown, and when the blood starts to run, turn them over and cook them for just another minute or so before adding a seasoning of salt and pepper, the paprika and the vegetables. Then pour in the wine and let it bubble and reduce slightly (for about 2 minutes). Then—off the heat—stir in the soured cream until you have a nice smooth sauce. Serve the liver straight from the pan onto pre-heated plates, with the onion, pepper and sauce spooned over it. This is delicious served with brown rice and some fried shredded cabbage.

Liver in yoghurt and juniper sauce

(serves 4 people)

| 1 lb lambs' liver (450 g)—ask the butcher to slice it very thinly |
| 1 largish onion |
| 1 clove garlic, crushed |
| 2 oz butter (50 g) |
| 1 teaspoon olive oil |
| 1 heaped teaspoon juniper berries, crushed |
| 5 fl oz natural yoghurt (150 ml) |
| Salt and freshly-milled black pepper |

First prepare the liver by cutting it into very thin strips, about 1½ inches (4 cm) long. The onion should be peeled, cut in half and then sliced thinly and the slices separated into little half-moon shapes. Now take a thick frying pan, melt the butter and oil together over a low heat until foaming, then add the onion, juniper and crushed garlic.

Cook them gently, without browning, for about 10 minutes. Now add the pieces of liver, increasing the heat, and brown them quickly and evenly by turning them—be careful not to overcook them. When they're browned, turn the heat right down again, take the pan off the heat and add the yoghurt—stirring it down into the pan juices—then return to the gentle heat and let it all simmer very, very gently for about 5 minutes. Taste, season with salt and freshly-milled black pepper, then serve the liver and sauce with rice and a side-salad.

Note: the cooked yoghurt sometimes takes on a slightly separated appearance but this is normal and in no way affects the flavour.

Ox liver and bacon hotpot

(serves 4 people)

This is another economical family supper dish—just 1 lb (450 g) of ox liver will be plenty for four people.

1 lb ox liver (450 g), cut into slices no more than ¼ inch (½ cm) thick
4 oz streaky bacon, rind removed and cut into small pieces (110 g)
1 medium-sized carrot, peeled and cut into chunks
1 celery stalk, cut into chunks
2 oz swede, peeled and cut into chunks (50 g)
3 fairly big onions, peeled and sliced
2 lb potatoes, peeled and cut into fairly thick slices (900 g)
1 heaped tablespoon seasoned flour
1 level teaspoon dried sage
1 teaspoon Worcestershire sauce
Stock or water
A little beef dripping
Salt and freshly-milled black pepper

Pre-heat the oven to gas mark 3, 325°F (170°C)

First of all, toss the slices of liver in the seasoned flour to coat them well, then arrange them in a good-sized casserole and sprinkle in any left-over flour. Then add the bacon and sliced onion, together with the chunks of carrot, celery and swede. Add the sage and a good seasoning of salt and pepper. Next pour in just enough stock or water barely to cover the ingredients in the pot— probably about 1 pint (570 ml)—then add the Worcestershire sauce. Finally, cover the top with a thick layer of potatoes, overlapping each other, then season again with salt and pepper. Cover the casserole and cook in the oven for 2 hours. After that, take the lid off and cook for a further 30 minutes.

When the time's up, brush the potatoes with a little melted beef dripping or butter and pop the casserole under a pre-heated hot grill to get a nice crusty top to the potatoes.

Faggots and peas

(serves 4 people)

A real old-fashioned treat—traditionally served with 'mushy' peas.

4 oz unsmoked bacon (110 g), bought in one piece, then cut into 1 inch (2·5 cm) cubes
1 lb pig's liver (450 g), cut into 1 inch (2·5) cubes
6 oz fat belly pork (175 g), cut into 1 inch (2·5 cm) cubes
2 medium-sized onions, quartered
15 fl oz stock (425 ml)
¼ teaspoon dried thyme
¾ teaspoon dried sage
¼ teaspoon powdered mace
2 oz fresh white breadcrumbs (50 g)
Salt and freshly-milled black pepper

For the mushy peas:
12 oz green split peas (350 g)
1 onion, quartered
1¼ pints water (725 ml)
1 teaspoon Worcestershire sauce
1 teaspoon tomato purée
1 dessertspoon mushroom ketchup
2 oz butter (50 g)
Salt and freshly-milled black pepper

Pre-heat the oven to gas mark 5, 375°F (190°C)

First of all, place the cubes of bacon, liver and pork in a casserole along with the quartered onions, then pour in the stock. Cover the casserole and cook in the centre of the oven for 45 minutes, then drain the meat and onions in a sieve (reserving the liquid). Next, using the fine blade of a mincer, mince the meat and onions into a mixing bowl, then add the breadcrumbs, herbs and spice. Season with salt and pepper, and mix to combine everything thoroughly. Next use your hands to shape the mixture into 8 good-sized balls.

Grease a shallow baking dish, and arrange the faggots in a single layer in it, pour over ½ pint (275 ml) of the reserved liquid, and bake (uncovered) on a high shelf of the oven for 45 minutes.

·To cook the peas: mix the tomato purée, Worcestershire sauce and ketchup with the water, and pour this into a pan, adding the onion quarters. Bring to the boil, then add the split peas and bring back to the boil. Now turn the heat down, cover the pan and simmer gently for ¾–1 hour, or until the peas are absolutely tender. After that, mash the butter into them, along with a seasoning of salt and pepper. If they seem a bit on the dry side, you can mix them with a bit of the stock left over from the faggots. Serve the peas with the faggots, and the juices poured over.

Lambs' kidneys in red wine

(serves 2 people)

6 small lambs' kidneys
1 large onion, chopped
12 oz dark-gilled mushrooms (350 g)
4 rashers unsmoked bacon, chopped
1 clove of garlic, crushed
1 level tablespoon flour
½ teaspoon fresh chopped thyme (or ¼ teaspoon dried)
½ pint red wine (275 ml)
2 oz butter or dripping (50 g)
Salt and freshly-milled black pepper

Begin by melting the fat in a pan and softening the onion and garlic in it for 5 minutes. After that add the chopped bacon and the mushrooms, and cook for a further 10 minutes. Meanwhile prepare the kidneys: cut them in half and remove the skins, then snip out the cores with a pair of kitchen scissors.

Now add the halved kidneys to the pan and cook them to colour a little, stirring them around the pan. Next sprinkle in the flour and stir it to soak up the juices, then add the thyme and pour in the red wine. Bring the whole lot to simmering point; season with salt (not too much, because of the bacon) and pepper. Then cover the pan and simmer gently for 15 minutes. Then remove the lid and simmer for a further 10 minutes.

Kidneys in fresh tomato sauce

(serves 2 people)

These are nice served with hot, buttery noodles and a green salad.

6 lambs' kidneys
12 oz ripe, red tomatoes (350 g)
1 medium onion, chopped
1 clove garlic, crushed
1½ teaspoons fresh chopped basil (or ¾ teaspoon dried)
1 level tablespoon tomato purée
1 level dessertspoon flour
1½ tablespoons olive oil
Salt and freshly-milled black pepper

Prepare the kidneys by peeling off the skins, cutting them in half and snipping out the white cores with some scissors. It's important to take out the cores—if you don't, the kidneys will be tough.

In a medium-sized saucepan, cook the onion gently in the olive oil for 6 minutes or so. Meanwhile pour boiling water over the tomatoes, slip the skins off and chop up the flesh roughly. Now add the kidneys to the onion, turn up the heat a little and let the kidneys brown, stirring them and turning them around. Next sprinkle in the flour and cook it for a minute or two, then add the chopped tomatoes, tomato purée and garlic. If you are using dried basil add it now, but if it's fresh keep it on one side. Have another good stir, season with salt and pepper, cover the saucepan and let it simmer over a gentle heat for about 20 minutes. Stir in the fresh chopped basil just before serving.

Curried lambs' kidneys

(serves 2 people)

This can be made with 2 pork kidneys, chopped, instead of lambs' kidneys.

6 lambs' kidneys
1 level teaspoon ground ginger
1 clove garlic, crushed
½ teaspoon chilli powder
1 level teaspoon turmeric
1 level teaspoon ground cumin
1 level teaspoon ground coriander
1½ tablespoons groundnut oil
1 large onion, very finely chopped

| 1 dessertspoon tomato purée |
| 5 fl oz water (150 ml) |
| 2 rounded tablespoons natural yoghurt |
| Salt and freshly-milled black pepper |

Begin by snipping the skin off the kidneys, then halve them lengthwise and cut out the white cores using some kitchen scissors. Now cut each kidney half into three or four pieces. Then, in a bowl, mix the garlic and all the spices together, add the kidney pieces and stir to coat them well. Cover the bowl with foil and leave to stand for an hour or so at room temperature.

After that, heat the oil in a wide, solid-based saucepan and soften the onion in it until it just begins to brown; then turn the heat right up, add the kidney pieces and toss them around to brown quickly. Next mix the tomato purée with the water and gradually stir this into the kidney mixture. Then season with salt and pepper, cover the pan and simmer very gently for 30 minutes, stirring once or twice. When the cooking time is up, taste to check the seasoning. Beat the yoghurt until smooth, and stir it into the kidney mixture over a gentle heat. Leave on the heat just long enough to heat the yoghurt through, then serve with spiced pilau rice and chutney.

Kidneys in jacket potatoes

(serves 4 people)

This is a lovely combination of kidney and bacon juices soaked into the potato.

| 4 large potatoes |
| 4 lambs' kidneys, skinned and cored |
| 8 rashers streaky bacon |
| A little made-up English or Dijon mustard |
| 2 oz butter (50 g) |
| Oil |
| Salt and freshly-milled black pepper |

Pre-heat the oven to gas mark 5, 375°F (190°C)

Clean the potatoes by wiping them with a damp cloth—or if they're very dirty—by scrubbing them. Then dry them as well as possible (if you wash them sufficiently early, you can leave them to dry for an hour or two). Rub the lightest film of oil into the skins of the potatoes (this makes them crisp), then bake them in the oven for 1–1½ hours, depending on their size. Test with a skewer to see if they're cooked.

When the potatoes are cooked, remove them from the oven and turn up the heat to gas mark 6, 400°F (200°C). Holding them in a cloth (they're very hot!) make an incision with a knife lengthwise and crosswise, and lift the four corners of skin up and pull them back a bit. Now make a depression in the centre of each potato, using a tablespoon. Season well with salt and pepper and add a knob of butter to each one. Then spread the rashers of bacon with mustard and wrap two round each kidney. Lay one in each potato and return to the oven for 30 minutes. Serve immediately, with a green salad on the side.

Curried ox kidneys

(serves 6 people)

Another very economical, yet rather special, curry.

2 lb ox kidneys (900 g)
2 large onions
2–3 tablespoons groundnut oil
1 tablespoon tomato purée
1 dessertspoon ground coriander
1 teaspoon ground turmeric
1 teaspoon cumin seeds
5 fl oz natural yoghurt (150 ml)
½ pint water (275 ml)
2 fat cloves garlic, crushed
About ½ teaspoon crumbled dried chillies, de-seeded
Salt

Begin by cutting the kidneys into pieces about 1 inch (2·5 cm) square, removing all the fat and cores as you do so. Then halve and thinly slice the onions (although this may look an awful lot of onion, it reduces to about half its initial volume).

Now heat the oil in a largish pan and, when it's sizzling hot, brown the kidneys, removing them to a plate afterwards with a slotted spoon. Stir in the onions and cook until they are golden brown, adding a little more oil if necessary. Now add the coriander, turmeric and cumin seeds and cook for a minute or two before stirring in the yoghurt and tomato purée, water and crushed garlic. Finally add the chillies and the kidneys. Season with salt, bring to simmering point, then cover and simmer gently for about an hour. Then take the lid off and continue to cook gently for a further 30 minutes or until the kidney is tender and the sauce thickened. Then serve on a bed of spiced rice, with an onion and tomato salad and some chutney.

Pork kidneys in mushroom and onion sauce

(serves 4–6 people)

1 lb (450 g) pork kidneys will serve 4–6 very economically, especially in this recipe which has lots of delicious sauce.

1 lb pork kidneys (450 g), (4–6 kidneys depending on size)

6 rashers streaky bacon, chopped

A little oil for frying

For the sauce:

1½ oz butter (40 g)

1 oz plain flour (25 g)

15 fl oz cold milk (425 ml)

½ lb mushrooms (225 g), very finely chopped

2 onions, very finely chopped

An extra 1½ oz butter (40 g)

Nutmeg

Salt and freshly-milled black pepper

Start by making the sauce. Melt the butter in a saucepan, then add the chopped onion and cook for 5 minutes to soften. Next add the chopped mushrooms, stir them in and cook—gently—for about 30 minutes without a lid or until the mixture is reduced to a pulp (give it an occasional stir to prevent it sticking).

Meanwhile make the white sauce by combining the butter, flour, milk and some seasoning in a saucepan and whisking it over a medium heat until it starts to bubble and thicken. Stir it (with a wooden spoon to get right into the corners), whisk again very thoroughly, then turn the heat down as low as possible and cook the sauce gently for 6 minutes.

When the mushroom mixture is ready, gradually stir the white sauce into it. Check the seasoning, add a good grating of whole nutmeg and then leave the sauce on one side while you prepare the kidneys.

First halve them, then using a pair of scissors snip out the cores and slice the kidneys across into bite-sized pieces. Now heat a little oil in a frying pan and add the chopped bacon and kidneys. Fry them over a medium heat until the kidneys are lightly browned (don't over-cook them or they will get tough—there should be just a hint of pink in the centre). Then stir the bacon and kidneys into the mushroom sauce. Re-heat gently, check the seasoning and serve with brown rice and a green vegetable.

Pork kidneys in chilli sauce

(serves 4 people)

The robust flavour of pork kidneys is well suited to a spicy sauce, like the one in this recipe.

6 pork kidneys
2 medium-sized onions, roughly chopped
1 large green pepper, de-seeded and chopped
1 clove of garlic, crushed
½ teaspoon dried chilli, crushed
1 tablespoon tomato purée
1 dessertspoon flour
1 × 14 oz tin Italian tomatoes (400 g)
3–4 tablespoons olive oil
Salt and freshly-milled black pepper

First prepare the kidneys by skinning them, halving them lengthwise and removing the core, then slicing them across into pieces about ¼ inch (½ cm) thick.

Now heat 3 tablespoons of olive oil in a good-sized casserole and brown the kidneys quickly over a high heat, then remove them to a plate. Next add the onion and green pepper to the oil left in the pan (you can add a little more oil if needed), and soften them for 5 minutes or so. Then stir in the garlic and the crushed chilli and cook for a minute or two more before returning the pieces of kidney to the pan.

Stir in the flour to soak up the juices, then pour in the contents of the tin of tomatoes, and add the tomato purée. Season well with salt and pepper, then simmer gently over a low heat for about 20–25 minutes without a lid. This is nice served with some rice and a salad.

Cold, pressed ox tongue

To press a pickled ox tongue yourself may sound a bit daunting but it's much easier than it sounds.

A pickled ox tongue, approximately 4–4½ lb (2 kg)
1 large onion, quartered
2 leeks, split and washed
2 carrots, cut into chunks
A few parsley stalks
6 peppercorns
A bayleaf
1 peeled clove garlic
2 teaspoons gelatine powder
2 tablespoons port

A 5–6 inch deep cake tin or soufflé dish (13–15 cm)

When you get the tongue home, scrub it well with a stiff brush then soak it for about half a day in cold water. Throw the water away and place the tongue in a deep pot, cover with 6–7 pints (3·5–4 litres) of fresh cold water and bring it to the boil. Now skim away all surface scum before adding the prepared vegetables, garlic, herbs and peppercorns. Simmer very gently for about 3½–4 hours.

The tongue will be ready when the skin along the surface is blistered and the 'T'-shaped bone at the root of the tongue comes away easily when pulled. Take the tongue out of the pot, then douse it with cold water and strip away all the skin. Trim the ragged and gristly bits of meat at the root and underneath the tongue to neaten it, then curl the tongue round and fit it into the tin or dish.

Now boil the cooking liquor briskly, to reduce it and concentrate the flavour a bit. Then sprinkle the gelatine into a little cold water in an old cup, melt it over simmering water until absolutely clear before straining it into ½ pint (275 ml) of the cooking liquor. Add the port and pour the mixture over the tongue. Put a saucer over, weight it heavily, then leave until cold and set. Serve the tongue with some chopped jelly as a garnish. This is delicious with pickles and chutneys or *Cumberland sauce*, see Part One, pages 156–157.

Right: Cold pressed ox tongue, this page; Damson ketchup, page 665; Spiced plum chutney, page 661; Quick pickled onions, page 667; Sweet piccalilli, page 664.

Lambs' tongue casserole

(serves 6 people)

Lambs' tongues make an excellent family casserole.

For the casserole:
2 lb lambs' tongues (900 g)
1 oz lard (25 g)
10 button onions, peeled but left whole
8 carrots, halved across
2 slices streaky bacon, chopped and rinds removed
4 oz mushrooms, halved if large (110 g)
1 oz plain flour (25 g)
½ pint stock—see below (275 ml)
½ pint dry cider (275 ml)
4 tablespoons fresh chopped parsley
Salt and freshly-milled black pepper

For the stock:
1 medium-sized carrot
1 medium-sized onion
1 stalk celery
1 bayleaf
1 bunch parsley stalks
6 peppercorns
Water

First of all, rinse the lambs' tongues in cold water, then place them in a large saucepan together with the vegetables and herbs for the stock (see ingredients). Season with just a little salt and pour over enough cold water to cover. Bring to the boil, cover the pan then simmer gently for 1½ hours. After that time, remove the lambs' tongues from the pan and continue to boil the stock—without a lid so that it can reduce. When the tongues are cool enough to handle, strip the skins from them and trim the bases (the discarded bits and pieces can go back into the pan while the liquid is reducing).

At this stage, pre-heat the oven to gas mark 3, 325°F (170°C). When the liquor has reduced to about ½ pint (275 ml), strain it into a measuring jug and make it up to 1 pint (570 ml) with cider.

Now heat the lard in a casserole, cut the tongues into slices about ¼ inch (½ cm) thick and fry these in the lard until browned—then remove them to a plate with a draining spoon. Stir the halved carrots and button onions into the fat remaining in the pan and let

Left: Kidneys in fresh tomato sauce, page 539.

these brown before adding the bacon and mushrooms. Cook them a little and return the slices of tongue to the pan.

Sprinkle in the flour, give it a good stir and cook for another couple of minutes before adding the stock and cider mixture. Bring it all up to simmering point, put a lid on the casserole and then cook in the oven for 1 hour. Taste and season if necessary, and just before serving, sprinkle in the chopped parsley.

Oxtail with haricot beans

(serves 4 people)

This is, I think, one of the best ways of cooking an oxtail as the beans absorb all the delicious flavour.

8 oz haricot beans, the long type (225 g)*
1 large oxtail cut into joints
2 medium-sized carrots, cut in chunks
2 medium onions, sliced
1 medium turnip, cut into longish chunks
2 large sticks celery, chopped
¾ teaspoon dried thyme, or a sprig of fresh thyme
¾ pint hot stock (425 ml)
¾ pint red wine (425 ml)
1 rounded tablespoon flour
2–3 oz beef dripping (50–75 g)
Seasoned flour
Salt and freshly-milled black pepper

* The beans should be either soaked overnight or covered with plenty of water, brought to the boil, simmered for five minutes then left to soak for 2–3 hours.

Pre-heat the oven to gas mark 2, 300°F (150°C)

Melt the dripping in a large frying pan until sizzling hot. Coat each piece of oxtail with seasoned flour and fry them to a really good nutty brown colour—then place them in a casserole. Next, fry the vegetables—adding more dripping to the pan if you need to—until they're nicely tinged with brown at the edges. Now add the vegetables to the oxtail along with the drained beans, stirring everything round a bit and adding the thyme.

Stir the flour into the juices left in the frying-pan and gradually add the stock a little at a time, followed by the wine (stirring constantly to prevent lumps). Season the sauce with freshly-milled pepper, but no salt as it can toughen the beans. Pour the sauce over the rest of the ingredients, put on a close-fitting lid and cook in the oven for 3 hours.

Before serving, spoon off any surface fat and season with salt, tasting as you do so. This is very good with braised red cabbage.

Sweetbreads with soured cream and onion sauce (serves 4–6 people)	2 lb calves' sweetbreads (900 g)
	½ teaspoon salt
	1 tablespoon lemon juice
	For the sauce:
	½ pint water (275 ml)
	2 large onions, sliced very thinly
	2 oz butter (50 g)
	¾ oz flour (15 g)
	½ teaspoon mustard powder
	5 fl oz soured cream (150 ml)
	Salt and freshly-milled black pepper
	A squeeze of lemon juice
	To garnish:
	Fried croûtons
	Chopped parsley

First, soak the sweetbreads in cold water for about 2 hours, changing the water fairly frequently. Then drain and place them in a saucepan with a further 2 pints (1·25 litres) of fresh cold water, and add the lemon juice and salt.

Now bring to the boil, reduce the heat to give a gentle simmer and cook for about 15 minutes. Drain the sweetbreads and douse with cold water. Now split them into pieces, removing any bits of tubes and tough outer membrane that you may come across. Then cover them and put them on one side.

Now to make the sauce: melt the butter in a large saucepan. When it is frothy, stir in the sliced onions and cook them over a very low heat for about 15 minutes until the onions are soft without being coloured. Then stir in the flour and mustard and cook for about 2 minutes before stirring in (gradually) the water. Bring to the boil, still stirring, then cover and simmer gently for 15 minutes.

Rub the contents of the pan through a sieve (or liquidise) until smooth. Now return the sauce to the rinsed-out pan, and stir in the cream. Return the sweetbreads to the pan and re-heat, very gently or the cream will separate. Then taste and season with salt, pepper and lemon juice. Now pour the lot into a warmed serving dish and surround with triangles of fried bread (croûtons). Garnish with chopped parsley and serve.

Tripe and onions

(serves 2–3 people)

2 lb tripe (900 g)
2 pints (approx.) light stock or water (1·25 l)
1 large carrot, cut into chunks
1 whole onion stuck with a clove
2 stalks celery, cut into chunks
Bouquet garni*
1½ lb Spanish onions, thinly sliced (700 g)
2 oz butter (50 g)
1 tablespoon oil
1–2 tablespoons cider vinegar
Chopped parsley, to garnish

* Bouquet garni: 1 sprig parsley, 1 sprig thyme, 1 bayleaf and 6 whole peppercorns tied up in a bag of muslin or doubled gauze.

First place the tripe in a large saucepan and pour in enough stock (or water) to cover, then add the carrot, whole onion and celery stalks, pop in the bouquet garni, bring up to boiling point, then cover and simmer for 30 minutes to an hour (this depends on how much blanching the tripe has had—your butcher should be able to tell you. It should still be a bit chewy after it has been simmered).

While the tripe is simmering, cook the sliced onions in 1 oz (25 g) butter and 1 tablespoon of oil in a large frying pan until golden but still slightly crisp. Then scrape the onions into a warmed serving dish and keep them hot.

Next drain the cooked tripe, dry it as much as possible then cut it into roughly 1 inch (2·5 cm) squares—discard the vegetables etc. Heat the remaining butter and fry the tripe until golden and lightly crisped. Cover the onions with the tripe, then pour the vinegar into the frying pan and swirl it round, scraping the base and sides of the pan—then pour the vinegar over the tripe. Sprinkle with the parsley and have extra vinegar on the table.

Cream and yoghurt

Including recipes for:

Since the western world has become involved in a seemingly endless dialogue on fats and their contribution to the causes of coronary heart disease, cream (along with butter, oils and other fatty foods) has inevitably come in for quite a battering. It goes without saying, however, that this chapter is not an invitation to everyone to eat lashings of cream regardless: moderation is always the last word. The fact is that cream is a natural food, and an ingredient to be used (with restraint) in cooking for which there is no really acceptable substitute. I would, for instance, rather have just one ice cream per year made from (guess what!) iced *cream*, than dozens made from synthetic, over-sweetened non-milk fat. For those who are forbidden cream, or are cutting down on their calories, then I would recommend they replace it with home-made yoghurt (see page 568)—which is utterly delicious and very different from the commercially-made kinds.

Cream

Without being too scientific about the subject, let's first consider the difference between the various types of cream. Butterfat is the name given to small globules present in milk, though not visible to the naked eye. Each one of these is surrounded by a layer made up of some of the other solid components in the milk. These little globules tend to gather together and rise to the surface of the milk, forming a layer. This layer is then skimmed off to become cream or butter.

The various types of cream are graded according to the amount of butterfat they contain. Thus *double cream* has to contain no less than 48% butterfat, *single cream* no less than 18%, and *half cream* no less than 12%.

Whipping (or ready-whipped) cream must contain not less than 35% butterfat. This, in fact, is the minimum requirement for whipping ability, which is the reason why single cream is unsuitable for whipping.

Clotted cream has the highest butterfat content of all (55%), and the clotting is achieved by a special treatment. The milk is scalded at a temperature of 180°F (82°C) and allowed to cool overnight before being skimmed. It is, as anyone who has had a holiday in the West Country knows, a real luxury.

There are of course other types of cream available: for instance, *UHT (ultra heat treated) cream*, packed in foil-lined containers, which keeps much longer than fresh cream, and *sterilised cream*, marketed in glass bottles, which lasts even longer. However the treatment that these products undergo to ensure their long life does affect their flavour. Unless there is absolutely no alternative, it is my opinion they are not worth using.

Soured (or cultured) cream

This is single cream (not less than 18% butterfat) which, when commercially-made, is heated and then inoculated with a culture. The temperature is controlled, and when the acidity reaches a certain level, clotting takes place. In Russia and some northern European countries cream was allowed to sour naturally for use in cooking, and many people have asked me if it is possible to sour cream at home. It's not, unfortunately, because all our bottled milk and cream is pasteurised, but it is possible to simulate it.

If you can't get soured cream you can simulate it by adding 1 teaspoon of lemon juice to 5 fl oz (150 ml) of single or double cream, depending on how creamy you want it. Leave it for half an hour or so, and it will have begun to thicken. Another, quicker, way is simply to combine in equal quantities cream (single or double) and natural yoghurt.

Soured cream is particularly useful in recipes, giving them a distinctive flavour (sharper than cream, but creamier than yoghurt). When you're buying it, it's important to look carefully at the date stamp, and make sure the expiry date is as far off as possible. Soured cream becomes more acid the older it gets. It *will* keep for about a week in the refrigerator, but bear in mind the flavour will be that much sharper.

Eggs en cocotte with soured cream and asparagus

(serves 6 people)

This is a lovely way to make a little asparagus go a long way, and its delicate flavour is just right with soft creamy eggs.

8 oz asparagus (225 g)
6 large fresh eggs
1 oz butter (25 g)
½ pint soured cream (225 ml)
6 heaped teaspoons freshly-grated Parmesan cheese
Salt and freshly-milled black pepper

Six 3½ in (9 cm) ramekin dishes, well buttered

Pre-heat the oven to gas mark 4,
350°F (180°C)

Steam the asparagus (see page 638) for just 4 minutes—it needs to
be only half-cooked. Then when it's cool enough to handle, chop it
into 1 inch (2·5 cm) lengths and arrange the pieces in the bases of
the dishes—making sure each one gets its fair share of the tips, but
also reserving six for the garnish.

Now carefully break an egg into each little dish, season it with salt
and freshly-milled black pepper, then gently spoon approximately
1 tablespoon of soured cream over each egg, spreading it out with
a knife so that it covers the top completely.

Dot them with flecks of butter and sprinkle each one with a
teaspoon of Parmesan cheese and place an asparagus tip in the
centre (all this can be done well in advance if you like).

To cook, pour about an inch (2·5 cm) of boiling water into a meat
roasting tin, place the dishes in it, pop the whole lot in the oven
and bake for about 15–18 minutes. Bear in mind, however, that
the eggs will go on cooking in the heat from the dishes on the way
to the table. Serve with buttered wholemeal bread and chilled
white wine.

Leek and soured cream flan

(serves 4–6 people)

This flan has a very crisp, cheese,
wholewheat pastry and makes a very
good lunch dish with a salad.

For the pastry:
3 oz self raising flour (75 g)
3 oz wholewheat flour (75 g)
¾ teaspoon mustard powder
A pinch of salt
1½ oz lard (40 g)
1½ oz margarine (40 g)
2 oz Cheddar cheese, finely grated (50 g)

For the filling:
3 lb leeks (1 k 350 g), trimmed with 1½ inches (4 cm) of green left on, then sliced thinly
1 clove garlic, crushed
2 oz butter (50 g)

1 large egg, beaten
5 fl oz soured cream (150 ml)
2 tablespoons double cream
2 oz grated Cheddar cheese (50 g)
Salt and freshly-milled black pepper

A 10 inch (25·5 cm) loose-based flan tin, greased

To make the pastry, sieve the flours, salt and mustard into a large bowl, then rub in the fats until the mixture resembles fine breadcrumbs. Now stir in the cheese, and add enough cold water to make a dough that leaves the bowl clean. Pop the pastry into a polythene bag and leave to rest in the fridge for half an hour.

Meanwhile pre-heat the oven to gas mark 4, 350°F (180°C), and put in a baking sheet to pre-heat as well. Roll out the pastry and line the flan tin, using any surplus pastry to reinforce the sides and base, carefully smoothing it into place. Prick the base all over with a fork, then bake the flan case in the centre of the oven on the baking sheet for 15 minutes. After that, remove from the oven and brush all over with a little of the beaten egg (from the filling ingredients). Return to the oven for 5 minutes more, then remove and turn the heat up to gas mark 5, 375°F (190°C).

Now for the filling: melt the butter in a large pan, add the leeks and garlic, and some seasoning. Cover and cook gently, without browning, for 10–15 minutes until they're sufficiently reduced to fill the flan case comfortably. Drain in a colander and return to the pan. Meanwhile combine the creams with the beaten egg and stir this into the leek mixture, seasoning to taste. Spread the mixture over the pastry case, sprinkle with the cheese and bake in the centre of the oven for 40 minutes, until brown and crispy.

Pork chops with cream and mushrooms

(serves 6 people)

This recipe is one of the most popular ones I've ever given. It's excellent for a dinner party because it doesn't need last minute attention.

6 large pork chops, trimmed of excess fat
12 oz mushrooms (350 g)
5 fl oz double cream (150 ml)

Juice of a large lemon
1½ tablespoons plain flour
2 teaspoons fresh chopped thyme (or 1 level teaspoon dried)
2 oz butter (50 g)
Salt and freshly-milled black pepper

Pre-heat the oven to gas mark 4, 350°F (180°C)

Place a large double sheet of cooking foil on a meat roasting tin, bearing in mind it must be large enough to wrap the chops in.

Now in a frying pan, brown the chops nicely on both sides in butter, and then transfer them onto the foil. Season each one with salt and freshly-milled black pepper and a little thyme.

Now chop the mushrooms roughly and fry them in the same pan in which the meat was browned, adding a little more butter if you think it needs it. Then pour in the lemon juice, let it bubble for a minute, then sprinkle in the flour and stir with a wooden spoon until you have a rather soggy-looking lump of mushroom mixture. Don't worry—it always looks awful at this stage.

Spoon the mixture over the pork chops, some on each, then spoon a little of the double cream over each one. Now wrap up loosely in foil, sealing it very securely, and bake them for 1 hour. Serve the chops with the delicious juices poured over. Since this is very rich, keep the accompanying vegetables fairly simple. A sprig or two of watercress beside each chop gives extra colour.

Note: when this is cooked the cream takes on a slightly curdled appearance, but this doesn't in any way spoil the delicious flavour.

Pheasant with cream and apples

(serves 2 people)

A hen pheasant is best for this recipe, which will only serve two, but you can, of course, double or treble the list of ingredients for more people.

1 plump young pheasant (oven-ready)
1 tablespoon butter
1 tablespoon oil
Half an onion, chopped small

3 medium-sized Cox's apples
About 6 fl oz dry cider (170 ml)
5 fl oz double cream (150 ml)
Salt and freshly-milled black pepper

First, heat the butter and oil together in a casserole. Then season the pheasant with pepper and salt and brown in the hot fat, turning it frequently so it browns evenly all over. Add the onion and let them soften gently whilst you quarter, core, and peel the apples. Slice them, not too thinly, and stir them into the casserole. Then add the cider, turn the bird onto its side and cover the casserole. Cook over a very low heat for about 1 hour or so, remembering that half-way through the cooking time you will have to turn the bird onto its other side.

Then, when the bird is cooked, remove it to a warmed serving dish. Simmer the apples remaining in the casserole until almost all the liquid has evaporated. Stir in the cream and season with salt and freshly-milled black pepper. Heat gently, then pour the apples and cream over the pheasant and serve.

Eighteenth century creamed apple flan

(serves 6 people)

This recipe is a nostalgic one for me as it's one of the first I tried after some research at the British Museum into 18th century British cooking, and it prompted me to do a whole lot more!

For the pastry:
4 oz plain flour, sifted (110 g)
1 oz margarine (25 g)
1 oz lard (25 g)
Water to mix

For the filling:
4 large cooking apples, peeled, cored and sliced
2 tablespoons water
2 oz butter (50 g)
2 tablespoons caster sugar
3 digestive biscuits, crushed into crumbs with a rolling pin

2 tablespoons brandy
The grated peel of a small lemon
2½ fl oz double cream (65 ml)
3 egg yolks
Freshly-grated nutmeg

Pre-heat the oven to gas mark 4, 350°F (180°C)

An 8 inch (20 cm) flan tin, lightly greased

Make up the pastry by rubbing the fats into the sifted flour until the mixture resembles breadcrumbs. Then add enough water to make a dough that leaves the bowl clean. Pop the pastry in a polythene bag and leave to rest in the fridge for 20 minutes or so, then roll it out and use to line the flan tin. Prick the base all over with a fork, and bake it for 20 minutes.

Meanwhile put the sliced apples in a saucepan with the water and cook until they are pulpy. Transfer them to a large mixing bowl and beat until you have a smooth purée. Then whisk in the butter and the caster sugar, followed by the biscuit crumbs, lemon peel and brandy, and a good grating of nutmeg. Combine everything thoroughly and leave the mixture to cool. Next whisk in the egg yolks together with the cream—don't over-do it, you just want to thicken it slightly. Then when the apple mixture has cooled, stir the eggs and cream into it. Pour the whole lot into the partly cooked flan case, then bake in the oven for a further 30 minutes.

Note: you can, if you like, substitute cider for the brandy.

Plum and soured cream flan

(serves 4–6 people)

Since I've been writing recipes, this is one I've found to be most popular with everyone who makes it.

6 oz shortcrust pastry (175 g) i.e. made with 6 oz (175 g) flour and 3 oz (75 g) fat
1 lb dessert plums (450 g)
½ pint soured cream (275 ml)
1 oz caster sugar (25 g)
3 egg yolks

½ teaspoon mixed spice

2 oz demerara sugar (50 g)

1 teaspoon ground cinnamon

Pre-heat the oven, and a baking sheet, to gas mark 6, 400°F (200°C)

A 10 inch fluted flan tin (25·5 cm), greased

Roll out the shortcrust pastry and line the flan tin, then halve the plums and remove the stones. Now beat the soured cream together with the caster sugar, egg yolks and mixed spice, then pour this into the flan case and arrange the plums over the top (flat side up). Place the flan on the baking sheet and bake for 20 minutes.

Then mix the cinnamon with the demerara sugar and sprinkle it all over the top. Bake for a further 20 minutes, turning the heat right up to gas mark 8, 450°F (230°C) for the final 5 minutes so that the top can brown nicely. Serve warm or cold.

English rhubarb fool

(serves 4 people)

Rhubarb fool has always been one of my favourite English puddings. You'll find all manner of recipes for it—but it's best of all when it's made with a proper custard, like this one.

2 lb rhubarb, washed and cut into chunks (900 g)

2 oz caster sugar (50 g)

1 teaspoon ground ginger

For the custard:

8 fl oz double cream (225 g)

3 egg yolks

1 tablespoon caster sugar

1 teaspoon cornflour

2 drops vanilla essence

To decorate:

4 pieces of preserved ginger cut into tiny chunks

First of all put the chunks of rhubarb, together with the caster sugar, into a saucepan then sprinkle in the ginger. Cover the saucepan and cook the rhubarb very gently for 15–20 minutes, stirring frequently (you want the rhubarb to be tender but not mushy). Then place the cooked rhubarb in a sieve over a bowl to drain off some of the juice.

Meanwhile make the custard. Bring the double cream up to boiling point in a small saucepan. Mix the cornflour, sugar, egg yolks and vanilla essence together in a basin until smooth. Pour the boiling cream onto the mixture, whisk thoroughly, then return the whole lot to the saucepan and back onto a medium heat. Carry on whisking until it has thickened, then immediately pour the custard into a bowl to cool (if it looks a little granular you can get it smooth again by beating). Now mash the drained rhubarb until smooth and combine it evenly with the custard. Pour this mixture into four serving dishes (stemmed glasses look nice), top with pieces of preserved ginger, cover with clingfilm and chill slightly before serving.

Rich lemon cream with frosted grapes
(serves 12 people)

This is the very nicest lemon dessert I've ever come across. It serves about 12 people, so is very good for a party. For a smaller quantity, use a 6 inch (15 cm) tin, 1 level dessertspoon gelatine, 1 egg yolk and half the remaining ingredients.

5 fl oz milk (150 ml)
4 level tablespoons caster sugar
Grated rind and juice of 4 lemons
1 level tablespoon powdered gelatine
1 egg yolk
1¼ pints double cream (700 ml)
4 large egg whites

To decorate:
4 oz white grapes (110 g)
1 egg white
Caster sugar

An 8 inch (20 cm) round cake tin, lightly oiled

Place the milk, sugar, grated lemon rind, gelatine and egg yolk together in a blender or liquidiser. Blend for half a minute at top speed, then pour the mixture into a small saucepan, and stir over a very gentle heat for 3 or 4 minutes until fairly hot but *not* boiling. Now return the mixture to the liquidiser and whizz round again, adding the lemon juice and ½ pint (275 ml) of the cream. When all is thoroughly blended, pour the mixture into a bowl, cover with foil and chill, stirring occasionally until the mixture is syrupy.

Whip the remaining cream lightly until it just begins to thicken, then in another very large bowl whisk the egg whites until stiff and carefully fold them into the lemon mixture, followed by the cream. Pour the mixture into the cake tin, cover and chill until firm.

To make the frosted grapes: first of all whisk up the egg white. Then break the grapes into little clusters of 2 or 3 grapes each and dip each bunch first in the egg white, then in a saucer of caster sugar. Leave them spread out on greaseproof paper for a couple of hours before using them.

Before serving, dip the cake tin for a moment in hot water, and turn the lemon cream over onto a plate. Decorate with the frosted grapes and serve the cream cut in slices rather like a cake.

Crème caramel

(serves 4–6 people)

A standard favourite with everyone from tiny babies to 90-year-olds.

5 fl oz milk (150 ml)
½ pint single cream (275 ml)
4 large eggs
1½ oz soft brown sugar (40 g)
1 tablespoon water, tap hot
4 oz granulated or caster sugar (110 g)
Vanilla essence

Pre-heat the oven to gas mark 2, 300°F (150°C)

A 1½ pint (850 ml) oval or round shallow baking dish

First put the granulated (or caster) sugar in a medium size saucepan and heat. When the sugar begins to melt, bubble and darken, stir and continue to cook until it has become a uniform liquid syrup, about two shades darker than golden syrup. Take the pan off the heat and cautiously add the water—it will splutter and bubble quite considerably but will soon subside. Stir and, when the syrup is once again smooth, quickly pour it into the base of the dish, tipping it around to coat the sides a little.

Now pour the milk and cream into another pan and leave it to heat gently while you whisk together the eggs, brown sugar and a few drops of vanilla essence in a large bowl. Then, when the milk is steaming hot, pour it onto the egg and sugar mixture, whisking until thoroughly blended. Then pour the liquid into the dish and place it in a large roasting tin. Transfer the tin carefully to the oven, then pour cold water into it to surround the dish up to two-thirds its depth. Bake for 1 hour. Cool and chill the crème caramel until you're ready to serve it. Free the edges by running a knife around before inverting it onto a serving plate.

Crème brulée

Crème brulée has its origins in England—it was invented at Trinity College, Cambridge where it was known as Burnt Cream. This could be called a cheat's version, but really it isn't. It has merely been adapted to help those who (like me) have never had a domestic grill that is suitable for fast caramelising of sugar. So here the caramel is made separately and simply poured over.

1 pint double cream (570 ml)
6 egg yolks
2 tablespoons caster sugar
4 level teaspoons cornflour
A few drops pure vanilla essence
6 oz granulated sugar (175 g)

Six ramekins, 3 inches (7·5 cm) diameter

You need to start the recipe the day before, so that the custard can be well chilled and firm. Heat the cream until it reaches boiling point, and while it's heating blend the egg yolks, cornflour, caster sugar and vanilla essence in a bowl. Then pour the hot cream in, stirring all the time with a wooden spoon, then return the mixture to the saucepan. Heat very gently (still stirring) until the sauce has thickened—which should only take a minute or two. (If it does overheat, don't worry—if you remove it from the heat and continue to beat it *will* become smooth again as soon as it cools.) Divide the custard between the six ramekins and leave to cool. Then cover each dish with clingfilm and refrigerate overnight.

About an hour before serving make the caramel. Place the granulated sugar in a heavy pan, then place the pan over a very low heat to dissolve the sugar gently and caramelise it (to get all the sugar to melt, just shake and tilt the pan from side to side, but don't stir). When all the sugar has dissolved and you have a clear syrup (about 10–15 minutes) remove the pan from the heat and pour immediately over the custards, covering the surface of each one. Now just leave them for a few minutes for the caramel to harden. Before eating the crème brulée, tap the surface of the caramel with a spoon to crack and break it up.

Note: to remove any hardened caramel from your pan, fill it with hot water and bring it to the boil.

Vanilla ice cream

You can of course buy electric ice cream gadgets and sorbetiers, but I don't think they're worth the extra expense. The freezing compartment of the fridge will do, provided it is turned down to its coldest setting about half an hour before you start to freeze the ice cream.

5 fl oz single cream (150 ml)
5 fl oz double cream (150 ml)
1½ oz caster sugar (40 g)
2 slightly rounded teaspoons custard powder
3–4 drops pure vanilla essence
4 egg yolks

1 polythene box, approximately 1½ pints (850 ml) capacity, with lid

First of all whip the double cream until it reaches the 'floppy' stage but isn't too thick, then pop it into the fridge to chill. At the same time put the polythene box into the freezer to chill as well.

Now make the custard by first pouring the single cream into a saucepan and then heating it up to boiling point. While that's happening beat together the egg yolks, vanilla essence and custard powder and sugar until absolutely smooth. Next pour the hot cream onto this mixture, whisking with a fork as you pour. Now return the custard to the pan and continue to whisk it over a medium heat until it has thickened and comes up to boiling point again. (Ignore any curdled appearance, which may come about if you don't keep stirring and have the heat too high. The custard powder will stabilise it provided you beat it off the heat: poured into a bowl it *will* become quite smooth again.)

Now place the bowl of custard in a bowl of cold water, and stir it now and then until absolutely cold. Then fold in the chilled whipped cream. Pour the whole lot into the chilled polythene box, cover and freeze for a couple of hours or until it is just beginning to set. At the same time place a mixing bowl in the freezer to chill, then as soon as the mixture does begin to set, tip it into the chilled bowl and whisk (with an electric hand-whisk or a rotary whisk) very thoroughly. Then return the ice-cream to the polythene box, put it back in the freezer (covered) and leave until frozen (about 3 hours). Before serving, remove the ice cream to the main body of the fridge for 45 minutes to get a smooth, not-so-hard texture.

Praline ice cream

1 quantity of vanilla ice cream (page 563)
2 oz unblanched almonds (50 g)
2 oz caster sugar (50 g)

Place the sugar and almonds together in a pan over a low heat, and leave them until all the crystals of sugar have completely dissolved to a liquid. Then cook until the liquid has turned a rich brown colour.

Then pour this mixture onto a well-oiled baking sheet, spreading the almonds out in a single layer. Leave the mixture to cool and become brittle then, using a palette knife, lift it off the baking tray onto a flat surface. Break it up with a few bashes from a rolling pin, then crush it fairly finely with the rolling pin.

Stir the crushed praline thoroughly into the ice cream about half an hour before serving. You can, if you like, make the praline at any time and store it in a screwtop jar, which will keep it crunchy.

Note: if you are short of time, the praline is also good just sprinkled over ice cream.

Blackcurrant ice cream

(serves 6–8 people)

I think blackcurrants make the very nicest ice cream, smooth, rich and velvety. However this same recipe works very well with loganberries, or even raspberries, if you prefer.

1 lb blackcurrants (450 g)
6 oz sugar (175 g)
5 fl oz water (150 ml)
½ pint double cream (275 ml)

A freezer-proof polythene box with a lid and a nylon sieve (a metal one can discolour the fruit)

There's no need to take the stalks off the blackcurrants, just pile them—about one-third of a pound (150 g) at a time—into the sieve set over a mixing bowl, and mash like mad with a wooden spoon until you have extracted all the pulp and only the stalks, pips and skin are left in the sieve. Loganberries or raspberries should be sieved in the same way.

Now place the sugar and water in a saucepan over a medium heat, stir until all the sugar crystals have dissolved, then let it come to the boil, and boil for 3 minutes exactly. Then remove from the heat and stir the syrup into the fruit pulp. Whip the cream until it *just* begins to thicken. Be careful not to overwhip—it mustn't be thick, just floppy. Fold the cream into the fruit mixture until thoroughly blended. Pour it into the polythene box, and freeze in a freezer or in the ice-making compartment of a refrigerator turned to its coldest setting.

As soon as the mixture begins to set (about 3 hours) turn it out into a bowl and beat thoroughly. Then return it to the freezer (in the box) until set, about another 3 hours. Remove to the main part of the fridge about an hour before serving.

Note: this ice cream should be eaten within 3 weeks.

Black Forest gateau

This is wickedly rich but not heavy at all. I think it makes a really lovely birthday cake for someone special.

6 large eggs
5 oz caster sugar (150 g)
2 oz cocoa power, sieved (50 g)
½ pint double cream (275 ml)
1 level tablespoon caster sugar
A 1 lb tin (or jar) morello cherries (450 g)
2 oz plain chocolate (50 g)
1 or 2 tablespoons kirsch (or rum)

Pre-heat the oven to gas mark 4, 350°F (180°C)

Two 8 inch (20 cm) sandwich tins, oiled with groundnut oil and the bases lined with greaseproof paper, also oiled

Start off by separating the eggs and placing the whites in a clean grease-free bowl. Put the yolks in another bowl and whisk them with the caster sugar until they just begin to pale and thicken (be careful not to thicken them too much, though). Now fold in the sieved cocoa powder.

Next, with a clean whisk, beat the egg whites until stiff but not too dry. Stir a heaped tablespoon of the egg white into the chocolate mixture to loosen it up a little bit. Then, using a metal spoon, carefully and gently fold in the rest of the egg white (trying not to lose any air). Divide the mixture equally into the prepared sandwich tins and bake them near the centre of the oven for about 15–20 minutes. They won't appear to be cooked exactly, just set and slightly puffy and when they're taken out of the oven they will shrink (but that's normal). Leave the cakes to cool in the tins, but turn them out while they're still faintly warm and strip off the base papers.

Now whip the cream with the tablespoon of caster sugar until it is a 'floppy', spreadable consistency. Next empty the tin of cherries into a sieve set over a bowl and combine 2 tablespoons of the juice with the kirsch or rum. Sprinkle this over the cake layers and, using a palette knife, spread about a third of the whipped cream over one cake.

Then slice the cherries and de-pip them (if they have any pips). Leave about a dozen whole ones for the decoration. Now arrange the sliced cherries all over the cake spread with cream. Next, carefully place the other cake on top and cover the entire cake with the remaining cream, again using a palette knife. Finish off by arranging the whole cherries around the edge, then grate the chocolate and sprinkle it all over.

Yoghurt

It's hard to believe that yoghurt—once a rather obscure substance to be found only in equally obscure healthfood shops—has become the staple snack of the 1980s. There appears to be no limit to the flavours of the month which turn up on the supermarket shelves; but it is just this that disappoints me about the many commercial brands. Despite all the invention which has been lavished on the sweetened flavoured varieties, they have failed to come up with a true *natural* yoghurt that bears much resemblance to what yoghurt should taste like. Let's look at the reasons for this.

What is yoghurt? It is a substance made from milk (whole, skimmed, evaporated or dried) which is first sterilised by heating to between 190°–221°F (88°–105°C), then cooled to between 106°–114°F (41°–45·5°C) and inoculated with a specially prepared culture. It is then incubated at a warm temperature until the acidity reaches a certain level and clotting takes place. After that it is cooled again, and is ready to eat or be stored.

In the Balkans and the Middle East yoghurt is made naturally from whole milk. This is boiled in open containers, which enable the milk to evaporate and reduce down to about two-thirds, or even half, its original volume. When it is made into yoghurt it is therefore thick, with a natural layer of cream on the surface. It also has a natural sweetness, like the sweetness of fresh milk, which it only loses as it ages and grows more acid. Commercially produced yoghurt is usually made with skimmed (low fat) milk and then thickened by the addition of powdered skimmed milk, rather than by reducing. So it doesn't have the creaminess of home-made natural yoghurt and the time taken in distribution means that it is fairly acid by the time it reaches our homes.

Home-made yoghurt I have already hinted that flavour is one reason for making your own yoghurt at home, but there are others. For one thing it is a great saving on the household bill (especially if you have a family that likes yoghurt), since the cost of making it at home is three or four times less than buying it. You can also be sure that the ingredients you use—and the flavours you add—are pure and natural. And equally important, it is so easy.

Making your own yoghurt

After a quite number of hit-and-miss yoghurt-making sessions (involving airing cupboards, warm blankets and the like) I was lucky enough to come across a method of making it at home— adapted by a man called Peter Bradford from the various methods he had studied in the Middle East—which involves just three items of equipment: a milk saver to prevent the milk boiling over, a cooking thermometer, and a wide-necked insulated jar. These items of equipment can be purchased as a yoghurt-making kit complete with a special yoghurt thermometer.

No electricity is needed, no warm cupboards and, best of all, after the initial stages, no effort on your part. The process works all by itself! The only ingredients required are 1 pint (570 ml) of milk and 1 teaspoon of natural yoghurt (as a 'starter' on the first occasion). This is the method:

Place 1 pint (570 ml) of milk in a fairly large, wide saucepan along with the milk saver (basically a small glass disc).

Bring it up to the boil, then let it simmer very gently for about 30 minutes, or until the milk has reduced to about 14 fl oz (400 ml), or roughly two-thirds of its original volume.

Now tip the reduced milk into a clean jug and place the jug in a bowl of cold water. Let the milk cool for 5 minutes, then place a clean dry thermometer in the milk.

If you're using a special yoghurt kit thermometer, wait until the mark reaches the red line: if you're using an ordinary cooking thermometer, wait until the temperature falls to 120°F (49°C). Now place ½ teaspoon of natural unsweetened yoghurt—a commercial brand will be alright—in the insulated jar, add a little of the milk, stir well, then add the rest of the milk, still stirring.

Next place the lid on the jar, and leave it like that for not less than 6 hours (or longer won't hurt).

Unscrew the lid, and inside you will have almost ¾ pint (425 ml) of delicious natural yoghurt for the price of 1 pint (570 ml) of milk. Replace the inner lid and store in the refrigerator.

Some important points Everything must be as clean as possible. And when you are washing out the jar before use, make sure it isn't still warm from the washing water: it must be room temperature.

Never use sweetened or flavoured yoghurt as a starter: it must be natural yoghurt. If you're making yoghurt continuously, you can in fact set aside ½ teaspoon of the previous batch to start the next, but every three months or so it is best to start with commercially made yoghurt (as this will have the right balance of culture).

Home-made yoghurt can be made with long life, skimmed milk or even powdered milk, but I think whole fresh milk makes the best.

Home-made curd cheese
This can be made from fresh yoghurt, and indeed the yoghurt kit mentioned above can be bought with a cheese-making nylon bag and stand. However, you can also assemble your own cheese-maker simply by placing a nylon sieve over a bowl and lining the sieve with a double piece of gauze (which is available at chemists' shops). This is the method:

Tip the freshly-made yoghurt into the nylon bag (or sieve) and allow the whey—the liquid content—to drain into the bowl beneath, leaving just the curd, or solid content, in the bag. After about 6 hours you will have a soft, creamy curd cheese which can then be used in exactly the same way as any other curd cheese or cottage cheese. You can, for instance, add some seasoning, garlic and fresh chopped herbs to it. I like it eaten Greek-fashion, chilled as a dessert with a spoonful of runny honey poured over.

Cooking with yoghurt
There are many recipes throughout the Cookery Course which make use of yoghurt. It does have a tendency to separate when subjected to heat and cooking, but this in no way affects the flavour (and myself, I'm not in the least bothered about the slightly granular appearance). If, however, you want to stabilise yoghurt for cooking, you can by blending 1 teaspoon of cornflour with a little cold water, mixing this with 5 fl oz (150 ml) of yoghurt, and simmering it for 10 minutes stirring all the time.

Serving yoghurt
Yoghurt with honey and wheatgerm
Serve thick yoghurt well chilled in stemmed glasses, with runny

honey dribbled over the top and a really generous sprinkling of wheatgerm over that.

Yoghurt with muesli

Place 2 tablespoons of muesli per person in bowls, then cover that completely with 2 tablespoons of thick yoghurt, and top with some runny honey.

Home-made fruit yoghurt

For the best results, use equal quantities of thick yoghurt and chopped fruit—strawberries, raspberries, blackcurrants or loganberries are all good. Add enough caster sugar or honey to sweeten according to your taste.

Dried fruit yoghurt

This is nicest of all made with prunes or dried apricots (or a mixture of both). Soak 4 oz (110 g) of apricots or prunes—or 2 oz (50 g) of each—overnight. Add 2 tablespoons of brown sugar and cook them for 10 minutes. Drain well in a sieve, then chop the flesh of the fruit and combine it with $\frac{1}{2}$ pint (275 ml) of thick yoghurt.

Yoghurt seafood sauce

(serves 4–6 people)

This is a lovely, piquant but very easy sauce to serve with shellfish—see, for instance, *Avocado and seafood salad* on page 520.

2 rounded tablespoons mayonnaise (see page 577)
4 tablespoons natural yoghurt, about 5 fl oz (150 ml)
1 tablespoon tomato purée
1 tablespoon Worcestershire sauce
2 level teaspoons horseradish sauce
2 tablespoons lemon juice
1 clove garlic, crushed
Cayenne pepper
Salt

This recipe is unbelievably easy, because all you do is combine all the above ingredients with a seasoning of salt and a pinch of cayenne, and stir well to blend them together thoroughly. Store, covered, in a cool place until needed.

Chilled yoghurt and cucumber soup

(serves 6–8 people)

This deliciously light and subtle soup is incredibly easy and quick to make. However it *does* need some fresh British cucumbers and not the rather tasteless imported ones.

1 medium-sized firm, young cucumber
5 fl oz natural yoghurt (150 ml)
2½ fl oz soured cream (65 ml)
A little milk
1 small clove garlic, crushed
1 teaspoon fresh lemon juice
1 level teaspoon fresh chopped mint
A few slices of lemon, cut very thinly
Salt and freshly-milled black pepper

First of all peel the cucumber thinly with a potato peeler so as to leave some of the green, then slice it. Reserve a few slices to garnish the soup, then place the rest in a liquidiser along with the yoghurt, soured cream and crushed garlic. Switch on and blend at the highest speed until smooth. Add a seasoning of salt and pepper and lemon juice, then pour the soup into a tureen and if it seems to be a little too thick, thin it with some cold milk. Now stir in the fresh chopped mint, cover with foil or with a lid and chill very thoroughly for several hours before serving.

To serve, ladle the soup into individual soup bowls and float a few thin slices of cucumber and a thin slice of lemon on each one.

Cucumber raita

(serves 4 people)

This is an accompaniment, or side dish, for serving with curries. The idea is that the coolness of the yoghurt and the cucumber will counteract the hotness of the curry and so it does—much more effectively than cold drinks.

2 oz peeled cucumber (50 g)
1 spring onion, finely chopped
½ clove garlic, crushed
5 fl oz natural yoghurt (150 ml)
2 pinches cayenne pepper

1 pinch cumin seeds
Salt and freshly-milled black pepper

First slice the cucumber thinly, then cut the slices in half, put into a basin and sprinkle with salt. Leave it for an hour, by which time a lot of the liquid will have been drawn out of it, so drain off the liquid and dry the cucumber in some kitchen paper.

Now combine the cucumber, yoghurt, spring onion and garlic, mixing them thoroughly. Season with salt and freshly-milled pepper. Pour the mixture into a serving bowl, sprinkle with cayenne and cumin, cover and chill thoroughly before serving.

Dried fruit salad with yoghurt and nuts

(serves 4–6 people)

If you're wholefood minded, you'll love this recipe, which is full of good natural things.

4 oz prunes (110 g)
4 oz dried apricots, separated (110 g)
4 oz dried figs (110 g) – cut out the hard stalk ends
4 oz large raisins, separated (110 g)
The zest and the juice of 1 orange
2 oz demerara sugar (50 g)
2 oz chopped, toasted hazelnuts (50 g)
15 fl oz natural yoghurt (425 ml)

The night before, place the four dried fruits in a deep 2½ pint (1·5 litre) bowl and cover with 1¼ pints (700 ml) cold water. Make quite sure *all* the fruit is immersed and leave to soak overnight.

The next day, drain off 3 fl oz (75 ml) of the water, then place the fruits, sugar and the remaining water in a small pan. Cover and bring to simmering point, and leave to simmer gently for about 10 minutes or until all the fruit has become tender when tested with a skewer. Next stir in the orange zest and juice, then tip the whole lot into a shallow serving bowl to cool. Cover with clingfilm and chill. Just before serving, spread the yoghurt carefully all over the fruit and sprinkle on the hazelnuts.

Salads and dressings

Including recipes for:
Vinaigrette dressing
Mayonnaise
Eliza Acton's English salad sauce
Green salad
Tomato salad
Green winter salad
Raw spinach and watercress salad
Rice salad
Brown rice and tuna fish salad
New potato salad with mint and chives
Red cabbage and coriander salad
Chick pea salad
Haricot bean and salami salad
Chinese beansprout salad with soy dressing
Four star salad
Broad bean salad
Salad Niçoise

I think it would be true to say that salads in this country were not all they should have been for a very long time; largely, I suspect, for the same reason our vegetable cooking lacked imagination: namely that our meat and fish were so good and plentiful that any other additions to the table took second place. Over a hundred years ago, a Victorian food writer described our lack of skill with salads as 'a defect in our national character'. He put it down to our obsession with pickles, and I think he had a point. Perhaps our delicious chutneys and pickles *are* to blame for that all-too-familiar sight a few years ago: wet lettuce leaves, tomato quarters and perhaps a radish presented alone and undressed, with only a bottle of the dreaded factory-made salad cream for company.

Well, times have changed and so have salads. They have been enlivened by the growth of foreign travel and a wider knowledge and interest in good food. Even stubborn grandmothers who swear they couldn't eat anything 'oily' will enjoy a really well-dressed salad (provided, you don't tell them about the oil!).

Salad dressings

The two most widely-used salad dressings are mayonnaise and vinaigrette, and indeed most other dressings are derived in some way from these two. It's the job of a good dressing to complement a salad rather than disguise it, and that's why the right ingredients are so important. This needs to be emphasised because the lack of them is the reason why so many dressings in so many restaurants are abysmal. So let's have a look first at the essential ingredients.

Vinegar As far as I'm concerned, malt vinegar should never find its way anywhere near a salad—its strong taste is too overpowering for delicate salad vegetables (I'm not decrying it: for pickling onions or sprinkling over fish and chips I wouldn't use anything else!). Salads need the much milder *Wine vinegar*, preferably the kind made by the slow Orleans method (see Part One, pages 176–177). The disadvantage of wine vinegar is of course its price, but *Cider vinegar* is also suitable for dressings and is less expensive.

You can also make your own *Flavoured vinegars* by adding sprigs of fresh herbs to steep in the vinegar. Tarragon is perhaps the best herb to use—and this is also a good way of conserving it for the winter, when a few drops of tarragon vinegar will give a dressing a nostalgic summery flavour.

Oil Olive oil is obviously the best choice, though its cost seems to get increasingly prohibitive. What few people realise, though, is the enormous saving that can be made by buying olive oil in bulk. It can be widely bought in 3, 4 or 5 litre cans (or polythene packs) which will save you pounds if you've been in the habit of buying small bottles from supermarket shelves.

Olive oil The best-quality olive oil comes straight from freshly cold-pressed ripe olives—this is called 'first pressing'. After that, there is usually a second pressing where the olives are heated in order to extract every last drop. The first pressing gives a fruity but mild taste: the second a stronger, often rather harsh one (sometimes if the olives were over-ripe it is too strong, and the oil has to be what one might call de-flavoured).

The only way to find an olive oil that suits you is to experiment. I have found that a good Italian olive oil is what I personally like best (the most famous is the kind produced in Lucca), though I've also had very good Greek olive oil made from olives from the Calamata region. Both of these can be purchased at Italian or Greek shops. When I can't get to one of them, I buy—again in bulk—a blended olive oil from a national chemist's chain-store, where the olive oil is now sold primarily for culinary rather than medical use, and has greatly improved.

Groundnut oil is always my second choice for salad dressings and, in fact, for mayonnaise it is my first choice. It is rich without having a pronounced flavour, but you do need to hunt around for it in specialised food shops or delicatessens. Maybe it will become more widely available if we keep nagging retailers for it!

Sunflower, soya and all other culinary oils can be used in salad dressings. These are strictly a matter of personal preference: when used for cooking some of them have a quite distinctive flavour, but when used cold are much milder and do not compete with the other flavours in a dressing. They are, for the most part, more economical than olive oil and therefore worth experimenting with.

Lemons Lemon juice, if liked, can be used instead of vinegar in a dressing. I once had a lovely salad in Greece made from olives, tomatoes, cucumber and Feta cheese, with fresh lemon juice squeezed straight on with a drizzle of olive oil. The combination was just right for that salad, though on the whole I have to admit that wine vinegar is preferable.

Vinaigrette dressing
The recipe I give, let me say straightaway, is a guideline rather than a rule. Not only do individual tastes differ, but the

ingredients can vary too. Sometimes a sharper dressing is what's required, sometimes a milder one. However I usually stick to the old saying: 'Be a counsellor with the salt, a miser with the vinegar, and a spendthrift with the oil.' This is good advice—the most common fault (especially in restaurants) is over-enthusiasm with the vinegar; and even worse I think, is the addition of sugar to counteract it. Anyway, my version is as follows:

Vinaigrette dressing	
	1 level teaspoon salt (English rock salt, crushed, is best for this)
	1 (or ½) clove garlic (according to taste)
	1 rounded teaspoon mustard powder
	1 tablespoon wine (or cider) vinegar
	Freshly-milled black pepper
	6 tablespoons olive oil

I like to start off with a pestle and mortar: first of all crush the flakes of rock salt to a powder, then add the peeled clove of garlic and pound that together with the salt—which will immediately bring out its juices and turn it into a smooth paste. Next add the mustard powder, vinegar and some freshly-milled pepper, and mix thoroughly until the salt dissolves. Finally add the olive oil, and just before dressing the salad, pour everything into a screw-top jar and shake vigorously to get it thoroughly blended.

I think salad dressings should be made as freshly as possible. So if you happen to have some left over, use it the next day but don't keep it any longer.

Note: there are any number of variations on this theme. For a *Vinaigrette with herbs*, for instance, add a teaspoon each of freshly chopped chives, tarragon and parsley just before serving.

Mayonnaise

No commercially-made mayonnaise, or short cut home-made version, can beat the thick, shining, wobbly texture of a proper mayonnaise you make yourself. For me, it's one of the true luxuries of the kitchen. Making mayonnaise for the first time can be a daunting experience, but *only* if the process is not explained properly. The following method is the traditional one and, I can assure you, pretty foolproof if you follow the instructions to the letter. At first it may seem a bit stupid to be adding the oil, literally drop by drop, and you'd be forgiven for thinking you're going to be there all night. The temptation to add more will be great. Don't, because the fact is, this method actually only takes 7 minutes from start to finish (yes . . . I've timed myself with a stopwatch).

Home-made mayonnaise	
	2 large eggs (yolks only)
	1 level teaspoon salt
	1 heaped teaspoon mustard powder
(makes ½ pint or 2·75 ml)	1 clove garlic, crushed
	½ pint groundnut oil (275 ml)
	White wine vinegar
	Freshly-milled black pepper

A 1½ pint (850 ml) basin, an electric mixer (or balloon whisk if you need the exercise), plus a damp tea-cloth for standing the basin on to keep it steady.

Begin by putting the egg yolks into the basin, then add the crushed garlic and sprinkle in the mustard powder, salt and a few twists of freshly-milled pepper: mix all these well together. Now with the groundnut oil in a jug in one hand, and your mixer or whisk in the other, add *one* drop of oil to the egg mixture, and whisk that in. However daft it sounds, this is the key to success—whisking each drop of oil in thoroughly, before adding the next. It's *not* going to take all day, because in a few minutes—after you've added several drops of oil—the mixture will begin to thicken. At that stage—and only then—you can begin to add the oil in larger drops (when the mixture has started thickening, the critical point is past).

When about half the oil is in, add about a teaspoon of vinegar to thin the mixture down. Now you can begin pouring the oil in a thin, steady trickle—whisking the whole time. When it's all in, taste and season with salt and pepper and, if it needs it, a little more vinegar.

Curdling occurs if you add the oil too fast at the beginning. If that happens, don't despair. Simply put a fresh egg yolk into a clean basin, add the curdled mixture to that (drop by drop), then carry on with the remainder of the oil as if nothing had happened. Mayonnaise should be stored in a screw-top jar in a cool place —the bottom of the fridge if you like—for no longer than a week.

Quick mayonnaise

For a quick (though not so thick) version of mayonnaise: place two *whole* eggs in a food processor or liquidiser and blend with the mustard, salt pepper and garlic (as in the previous recipe). Then with the motor turning, pour in all the oil in a steady stream. Taste and add vinegar at the end.

Mayonnaise forms the basis of a number of other sauces.

Aioli sauce

This is one of the best-known, and often served with fish or vegetables in the South of France. Follow the method above precisely, using 4 cloves of garlic instead of one (or more if you're a garlic addict!).

Sauce tartare

This is served with grilled or fried fish. Stir into the finished mayonnaise 2 finely chopped gherkins, 2 level teaspoons chopped capers, and 2 level teaspoons chopped parsley (or tarragon).

Sauce rouille

This is sometimes spread on baked croûtons of French bread and eaten with fish soups, or else stirred into the soup itself. It's also good served with any fried fish, or used as a dip for fried prawns for a first course. Make up half the quantity of *Quick mayonnaise* (see above), adding 2 crushed cloves garlic, 2 dessertspoons lemon juice (instead of the vinegar) 2 heaped teaspoons tomato purée, 2 level teaspoons paprika and 1 pinch cayenne pepper.

Eliza Acton's English salad sauce

(serves 4–6 people)

This sauce made with fresh cream and some cooked egg yolks makes a lovely dressing for potato, or for any other vegetable salad; it's good served with cold chicken, eggs or even fish; and with a little curry powder added it is ideal for a macaroni salad. The recipe comes from *Modern Cookery for Private Families* (modern that was, in 1845).

The yolks of 3 hard-boiled eggs
5 fl oz double cream (150 ml)
4 teaspoons white wine vinegar
1 tablespoon cold water

Right (from top to bottom): Lamb kebabs, page 602; American hamburgers, page 598; Rice salad, page 586; Bacon and egg pie, page 607.

2 pinches cayenne pepper
¼ **teaspoon salt**

Bring the eggs to the boil in plenty of cold water (they must be completely covered) and give them 9 minutes exactly from the time it starts boiling. Then run them under the cold tap to cool them— and stop them cooking any further. Peel away the shells and the whites, and place the yolks only in a mixing bowl.

Add a tablespoon of cold water and pound the yolks to a smooth paste with a wooden spoon. Then add a couple of pinches of cayenne plus the salt, and stir in the cream, bit by bit, mixing it smoothly as you go. When it's all in, add the vinegar and taste to check the seasoning. If you think the mixture's far too runny at this stage, don't worry. Cover the bowl and leave it for a couple of hours in the refrigerator, after which time it will have thickened (it should, in any case, have the consistency of thickish cream rather than mayonnaise).

Salad ingredients and their preparation

Lettuce I could never recommend one particular kind of lettuce, because I like to ring the changes in my salads, and each variety has a different charm of its own. However I do have firm opinions on how a lettuce should be treated, whatever the variety.

First of all I've found the best way to store lettuces is to remove the root but otherwise leave them whole, and enclose them in a polythene bag in the lowest part of the fridge. I believe washing should be avoided if possible, as once the leaves are wet it is so difficult to get them dry again. What I prefer to do is take a damp piece of kitchen paper and wipe each leaf, removing any specks of dust (and crawly things)—this way the lettuce leaves remain dry and can more easily be coated with dressing. Now I realise many people will not agree with me here and will want to wash the leaves: in that case plunge the separated leaves briefly into cold water and place them in a salad basket (see illustration in Part One, page 19), then either hang them up after a good shaking or else swing the basket round and round out-of-doors. Finish off by drying the leaves carefully with kitchen paper. Never use a knife when you prepare lettuce, because cutting tends to brown the edges of the leaves. Breaking up the leaves too soon can cause them to go limp quickly, so always leave them whole, if possible, until you're ready to serve the salad (and even then use your hands rather than a knife).

Left (from top to bottom): Hot herb and garlic loaf, page 600; Salad Niçoise, page 594; Chinese beansprout salad with soy dressing, page 591.

Chinese leaf This looks like a cross between a cabbage and a head of celery—thick white ribs edged with a green leaf. It is marvellous for winter salads when imported lettuces are thin and travel-weary. Just slice it whole, horizontally, as and when you need it, storing the rest in a polythene bag. The very stalky bits at the base, in fact, are delicious lightly fried and served as a vegetable.

Chicory These are tight little buds of very crisp leaves (sometimes white, sometimes a reddish colour). Since light spoils the leaves they are usually wrapped in tissue paper, and are best kept in this until needed. They can be braised and cooked as a vegetable, but I think are best sliced horizontally and used to give a salad extra crunchiness. The leaves are slightly bitter-tasting and therefore need a well-flavoured dressing.

Beetroot This is a salad vegetable that suffers either from having no flavour if it's served alone, or from being totally overpowered by malt vinegar. I prefer to buy it cooked, chop it up with a generous sprinkling of raw shallot or onion and serve it in a vinaigrette dressing. If you want to cook it yourself, it needs washing before boiling for $1\frac{1}{2}$–2 hours with root, skin and a little of the stalk intact (as it's important not to let any of the juice 'bleed' out). It's ready when the skin slips off easily.

Cabbage Most varieties of cabbage make good salad ingredients if the stalks are removed and leaves are very finely shredded. See *Red cabbage and coriander salad* on page 588.

Fennel A bulbous-looking vegetable, similar in texture to celery but with a distinctive aniseed flavour. Sliced raw and separated into strips in a salad it responds beautifully to a well-flavoured olive oil dressing or some very garlicky mayonnaise.

Cucumber There's nothing nicer than a firm, young cucumber eaten the day it's picked with its flower still intact at the end. However if you're obliged to buy a plastic-wrapped one, do try to feel whether the stalk end is soft—if it is, that cucumber's past its peak. I never peel cucumbers because, as with many other vegetables, I like the appearance and flavour of the skins. If you prefer to peel them, use a potato peeler (which will only pare off the outer skin). Ever since I discovered them on holiday in Greece I've loved the crunchiness of *Ridge cucumbers*. These are shorter and fatter than ordinary cucumbers with little prickles along the ridges. The tough skins of this variety do have to be peeled.

Spring Onions Finely chopped (including most of the green parts as well) these are the best onions for salads—or whole, to be taken on picnics and dipped in salt. Welsh onion—which resembles the green part of spring onion— grows happily in our herb bed through the winter, too. It has a stronger flavour than chives but, finely chopped, it makes an excellent winter substitute for chives.

Watercress I love watercress in a green salad, and now that it can be bought ready picked-over and vacuum-packed, it saves such a lot of time (even if it is a little more expensive). Inside the unopened pack, watercress will keep for about 5 days, but once exposed to the air it wilts extremely quickly. For this reason, if you use it for a salad or garnish, don't put it on until the last moment. Watercress bought in bunches should be first picked over and de-stalked, then stored upside down with the leaves submerged in cold water.

The well-dressed salad

I really wouldn't suggest that the French have the last word on everything in the kitchen, but when it comes to dressing a salad properly, we can certainly learn from them. In Italy a haphazard sprinkling of some vinegar, followed by the same of oil with no particular regard for proportions, has killed off many a salad I would have otherwise enjoyed there. (I once read of the owner of a taverna on one of the Greek islands who, with the aid of a sprinkler fixed to the top of a bottle, could aim the dressing for a salad from a distance of four tables away!) In England we have a chemical-tasting oddity called salad cream which often lurks amongst the naked ingredients.

The French, on the other hand, dress their salads with a lot of care—and care is the operative word. A green salad will be given a wide bowl, with ample room for tossing, so that each leaf will be coated and glistening. A tomato salad will be presented on a wide, shallow plate so that the slices don't overlap each other and become damp and woolly. The tradition at 18th century French dinner parties was for the salad to be dressed at table by the hands of the most beautiful lady present. And therein lies the secret of the well-dressed salad—not looks, but *hands*. I'm convinced this is the only way to dress a leafy green salad really well.

So a few points to remember: always have a roomy bowl with space to toss the salad well, sprinkle in a little dressing at a time—never pour it so that one leaf gets totally drenched, and toss the leaves with your hands gently and carefully, so they get evenly coated but never soggy. Use *only* enough dressing to achieve this: if you finish up with pools at the bottom of the bowl, you have failed.

Green salad

The nicest green salads are the simplest, those with the least ingredients: crisp, dry lettuce leaves alone, or perhaps with some watercress, a little finely-chopped spring onion (or shallot) and a plain vinaigrette dressing. Or possibly one with a few fresh chopped herbs added.

Tomato salad

A tomato salad needs careful preparation and, properly made, it makes a good starter before a meal served with some crusty French bread and fresh butter. Choose firm but ripe tomatoes. Pour some boiling water over them and in a minute or two the skins will slip off very easily.

Never prepare a tomato salad too far in advance, because once you slice tomatoes they go a bit woolly. Another important point is that you should use a large flat plate for them—or else smaller individual plates—because the slices shouldn't overlap each other, another thing that causes sogginess.

For my tomato salad I like to sprinkle on some very finely chopped raw onion and lots of fresh chopped parsley and perhaps a mere trace of sugar—and some fresh chopped basil leaves would be a luxurious addition. Do not dress the salad until the last minute before serving.

Green winter salad

(serves 4–6 people)

Crisp chicory and Chinese leaves with winter lettuce and an avocado make a delicious salad for the winter months when there is a shortage of fresh greens.

1 small lettuce
1 head chicory
Half a head Chinese cabbage
1 small onion
1 ripe avocado

For the dressing:
2 cloves garlic
1 level teaspoon mustard powder

1 level teaspoon salt
1½ tablespoons wine vinegar
4½ tablespoons olive oil

Select only the crispest leaves of the lettuce, wipe them and arrange them in a salad bowl. Discard any bruised leaves and hard stalk of the chicory, then slice it directly into the bowl in about ¼ inch (½ cm) slices (separating the slices). Now slice the cabbage in the same way, chop the onion fairly finely and add that too. The avocado should be cut from top to bottom, opened up and the stone removed. Now cut each half in half again, and with a sharp knife you should find the skin will peel away whole if the avocado's ripe. Then chop the flesh into ¾ inch (2 cm) squares and add to the salad. Toss it well.

Then make up the dressing: place the peeled garlic cloves, salt and mustard powder in a mortar and crush to a paste. Next stir in the wine vinegar, followed by the oil, then transfer to a screw-top jar and shake vigorously to amalgamate everything. Pour the dressing over the salad, mix to give it all a good coating and serve.

Raw spinach and watercress salad

(serves 4 people)

This salad is a meal in itself and makes a change from the inevitable lettuce.

8 oz young spinach leaves (225 g)
1 bunch watercress
2 hard boiled eggs, chopped
4 slices bacon, grilled until crisp

For the dressing:
4 tablespoons dry sherry
3 tablespoons olive oil
3 tablespoons wine vinegar
1 teaspoon lemon juice
Salt and freshly-milled black pepper

Wash the spinach and watercress leaves thoroughly first, and discard the stalks and any damaged leaves. Then dry them carefully in a clean tea towel (or salad basket)—do this a few hours ahead of time if you can, to be sure of getting them quite dry.

To make the dressing, whisk all the ingredients together in a basin, using a fork, or shake them together in a screw-top jar, then taste and season to your liking.

To make the salad, tear the spinach leaves into manageable pieces and place in a salad bowl with the watercress leaves. Pour the dressing over and toss the leaves thoroughly. Then garnish with the chopped eggs and the bacon crumbled into small pieces, and eat straightaway.

Rice salad
(serves 4–6 people)

This can, of course, also be made with white rice—in which case the rice needs to be cooked for just 15 minutes.

Brown rice, measured to the 10 fl oz level in a glass measuring jug (275 ml)
1 pint boiling water (570 ml)
1 dessertspoon oil
3–4 tablespoons vinaigrette dressing (see page 576)
3 spring onions, very finely chopped
2 inches cucumber, unpeeled and finely chopped (5 cm)
2 large tomatoes, skinned and finely chopped
Half a red or green pepper, de-seeded and finely chopped
1 red dessert apple, cored and chopped with the skin left on
1 oz currants (25 g)
1 oz walnuts, finely chopped (25 g)
Salt and freshly-milled black pepper

Heat the oil in a saucepan, then stir in the rice to get the grains nicely coated. Add some salt, pour the boiling water over and bring back to the boil. Stir once, place the lid on and simmer the rice gently for 40 minutes or until all the liquid has been absorbed (tilt the pan slightly to check if there's any water left).

Now empty the rice into a salad bowl, fluff it up with a fork and then pour the dressing over while it's still warm. Leave it to get cold, then mix in all the other ingredients, adding a little more dressing if you think it needs it, and tasting to check the seasoning. Keep in a cool place until needed.

Brown rice and tuna fish salad

(serves 3–4 people)

This is a salad I serve for lunch with plenty of crusty bread to go with it.

Long grain brown rice measured to the 8 fl oz (225 ml) level in a glass measuring jug
Boiling water measured to the 16 fl oz (450 ml) level
1 oz butter (25 g)
½ teaspoon salt
1 × 7 oz tin tuna fish (200 g)
1 tablespoon capers, drained
1 tablespoon fresh chopped parsley
1 teaspoon grated lemon rind
The juice of half a lemon
1 dessertspoon wine vinegar
1 teaspoon mustard powder
3 tablespoons olive oil
A few drops Tabasco sauce
A 2 inch piece unpeeled cucumber, finely chopped (5 cm)
Salt and freshly-milled black pepper

Melt the butter in a medium-sized pan, then stir in the rice so that it gets nicely coated with butter. Add the boiling water and salt, stir once only, then cover and simmer gently for 40 minutes. When the time's up, check that the rice is tender and there is no water left in the pan. Now tip the cooked rice into a wide shallow bowl and fluff it up with a skewer.

Next, in a screw-top jar, combine the oil, vinegar, mustard and lemon juice by shaking vigorously, then pour it all over the rice while it is still warm, then leave to cool. Meanwhile drain the tuna in a sieve set over a bowl, and break the fish into small flakes. When the rice is cool, add the tuna (plus one tablespoon of its oil), together with all the remaining ingredients. Mix thoroughly, taste and season well.

Serve this on crisp lettuce leaves, and have some lemon quarters to squeeze over and some cayenne pepper on the table.

New potato salad with mint and chives

(serves 4–6 people)

This potato salad is so good it's almost best to eat it on its own.

2 lb small new potatoes (900 g)
2 sprigs mint
8 medium-sized spring onions, very finely chopped
3 tablespoons fresh chopped mint
2 tablespoons fresh chopped parsley
2 tablespoons fresh snipped chives
Vinaigrette dressing (see page 576)
Salt and freshly-milled black pepper

Wash the potatoes but *don't* scrape them (there's a lot of flavour in the delicate skins of new potatoes). Place them in a saucepan with salt and a couple of sprigs of mint, then pour boiling water on them, enough to come about halfway up. Put on a tight-fitting lid and simmer them until tender, being very careful not to over-cook. About 20–25 minutes should be enough: test them with a skewer, they should be tender but firm. Over-cooking will make them watery and mushy.

Drain them in a colander, then put them in a salad bowl. Chop them roughly with a knife, and pour on the dressing while they're still warm. Mix thoroughly. When the potatoes have cooled, mix in the fresh herbs and chopped spring onions. Taste, to check the seasoning, and keep the salad in a cool place until needed.

Red cabbage and coriander salad

(serves 6–8 people)

This is an ideal winter salad and a good one for help-yourself parties.

8 oz red cabbage (225 g)
1 medium-sized Cox's apple
1 onion, finely chopped
2 sticks celery, finely chopped
For the dressing:
2 tablespoons wine vinegar
2 tablespoons olive oil
$2\frac{1}{2}$ fl oz natural yoghurt (75 ml)
$\frac{1}{2}$ teaspoon salt

½ teaspoon mustard powder
1 clove garlic
½ teaspoon coriander seeds, crushed
Freshly-milled black pepper

First of all, cut the cabbage into quarters, remove the ribby parts then shred the rest as finely as possible directly into a large mixing bowl. Then grate the apple (leaving the skin on) into the cabbage, and add the chopped onion and celery. Stir it around and get everything evenly distributed before making the dressing.

For the dressing, crush the garlic together with the salt, mustard powder and some pepper with a pestle and mortar (or in a basin using the end of a rolling pin), then pour in the oil and vinegar. Give it a good stir, then add the yoghurt and crushed coriander. Now mix vigorously with a fork to amalgamate everything, pour the dressing onto the salad and toss well.

Note: you can make and dress this salad well in advance as it keeps well in a polythene box stored in the refrigerator.

Chick pea salad
(serves 4–6 people)

Chick peas are nutty and slightly crunchy in a salad but you have to plan this one in advance because they must be soaked overnight.

8 oz chick peas, soaked overnight (225 g)
8 oz haricots verts, (thin green string beans) (225 g)
5 fl oz garlic-flavoured mayonnaise (150 ml)—see page 577
1 × 1¾ oz tin anchovy fillets, drained and finely chopped (45 g)
6 spring onions, finely chopped
2 tablespoons capers, drained and chopped
2 tablespoons finely chopped parsley
Lemon juice to taste
A dozen black olives, pitted and halved
A few crisp lettuce leaves
Salt and freshly-milled black pepper

Bring the chick peas to the boil and simmer until tender (about 1¼ hours). Don't salt the water though, or the chick peas will never soften! The topped and tailed green beans will need 3 or 4 minutes in boiling salted water, then tip them into a colander, rinse them with cold water, drain well and cut each bean in half.

Combine the mayonnaise, anchovy fillets, spring onions, capers, chopped parsley and a good seasoning of salt and pepper. Then fold the well drained and cooled chick peas with the green beans and black olives into the mayonnaise mixture. Taste, and add a little lemon juice and more seasoning if necessary. Serve piled on a bed of crisp lettuce leaves.

Haricot bean and salami salad

(serves 2 people)

Not simply a side-salad this one, but a pretty substantial lunch (or supper) dish on its own. The haricot beans I recommend for this are the long, thin variety (rather than the small 'baked bean' type).

8 oz dried haricot beans (225 g)
1 small onion stuck with 2 cloves
A few parsley stalks
1 bayleaf
1 clove garlic, crushed
¼ teaspoon dried thyme or a sprig of fresh thyme
2 oz Italian salami, finely diced (50 g)
1 small onion, chopped
2 tablespoons fresh parsley, chopped
Freshly-milled black pepper

For the dressing:
1 tablespoon red wine vinegar
1 teaspoon mustard powder
1 heaped teaspoon salt
1 clove garlic
5 tablespoons olive oil
Freshly-milled black pepper

First place the beans in a saucepan, add about 4 pints (2·25 litres) cold water, cover with a lid and bring to the boil. Then turn off the heat and leave the beans to soak for 1 hour. After that, add the onion stuck with cloves, the parsley stalks, bayleaf, garlic, thyme and a few twists of pepper. Bring the beans back to the boil and simmer gently, uncovered, for 1–1½ hours or until tender.

While the beans are cooking, prepare the dressing. Crush the garlic in the salt (with a pestle and mortar), and then mix in the mustard powder and some pepper, followed by the vinegar and the oil. Transfer the dressing to a screw-top jar and shake vigorously to blend the ingredients. (If you have neither a pestle and mortar nor a garlic press, place the peeled clove on a hard surface and crush it with the flat blade of a knife.)

When the beans are cooked, drain them and discard the onion, bayleaf and parsley stalks. Tip the beans into a large bowl. Pour over the dressing, then add the diced salami, onion and chopped parsley—mix gently to avoid breaking the beans. Taste and season, and leave to cool before serving.

Note: if you can't get Italian salami, use another kind.

Chinese beansprout salad with soy dressing

(serves 4–6 people)

This is a very bright and beautiful salad to look at and the unusual dressing makes it really different.

8 oz fresh beansprouts (225 g)
1 small red pepper, de-seeded and chopped
About 6 inches unpeeled cucumber (15 cm), diced
Half a bunch watercress
1 small onion, thinly sliced and separated into rings

For the dressing:
½ teaspoon ground ginger
½ small onion, finely chopped
6 fl oz olive oil, or for economy groundnut oil (175 ml)
2 fl oz red wine vinegar (55 ml)
2 fl oz cold water (55 ml)
2 tablespoons soy sauce
1 small stalk celery, chopped
2 teaspoons tomato purée
2 teaspoons lemon juice
Salt and freshly-milled black pepper

In a good roomy bowl combine the beansprouts, chopped pepper, diced cucumber and sliced onion. Pick over the watercress selecting the best leaves and add them to the salad. Cover the bowl with clingfilm and chill in the refrigerator while you make up the dressing. For this, all you do is simply place all the dressing ingredients in a liquidiser, and blend until smooth. Taste, and season the dressing as required.

For this salad I would suggest you serve the dressing separately in a jug, for people to help themselves.

Note: if you don't have a liquidiser, then combine the dressing ingredients by shaking them together in a screw-top jar.

Four star salad
(serves 4 people)

This salad is a meal in itself. The 'stars' in question here are avocado, garlic sausage, mushroom and lettuce with a lovely, garlicky, soured cream dressing.

2 ripe avocados
4 oz small pink-gilled mushrooms (110 g)
8 oz French garlic sausage, in one piece (225 g)
2 cloves garlic, crushed
1 tablespoon lemon juice
2 tablespoons mayonnaise
2 tablespoons olive oil
1 tablespoon wine vinegar
1 teaspoon mustard powder
1 medium-sized lettuce
4 spring onions, finely chopped
5 fl oz soured cream (150 ml)
Salt and freshly-milled black pepper

Begin by combining the soured cream with the garlic, mayonnaise and mustard powder. Then mix together the oil, vinegar and lemon juice and gradually add these to the soured cream mixture, tasting and seasoning with some salt and pepper. Now slice the garlic sausage into $\frac{1}{2}$ inch (1 cm) slices and then cut these slices into $\frac{1}{2}$ inch (1 cm) strips. Next break up the lettuce leaves and arrange them in a salad bowl: wipe and thinly slice the mushrooms (don't take the skins off) and add these to the lettuce pieces.

Finally prepare the avocados by removing the stones and peeling them, then cutting them into ½ inch (1 cm) cubes. Add these to the lettuce and mushrooms along with the strips of garlic sausage. Mix it all together gently, then add the dressing and toss again very gently. Sprinkle the chopped spring onions all over the surface and serve straightaway. This is nice served with *Home-made granary bread* which can be made by using the *Quick Wholewheat bread* recipe (Part One, page 51), made with half wholewheat flour and half granary flour.

Broad bean salad

(serves 2 people)

I devised this recipe when I had a glut of broad beans in the garden—now it's a firm favourite.

1½ lb broad beans (700 g), the weight before shelling
2 rashers lean bacon, rinded
1 tablespoon fresh chopped herbs (I use a mixture of tarragon, marjoram and parsley)
4 spring onions, finely chopped

For the dressing:
1 small clove garlic, crushed
1 teaspoon English mustard powder
1 dessertspoon lemon juice
1 dessertspoon wine vinegar
1 level teaspoon crushed rock salt
Freshly-milled black pepper
4 dessertspoons oil

First cook the bacon until it's really crisp, then drain it well and crumble it into very small pieces. Next make the dressing by dissolving the salt in the lemon juice and vinegar for a few minutes, then shake it with the rest of the ingredients in a screw-top jar to get everything thoroughly amalgamated.

Now cook the shelled beans in a very little salted water for about 5 minutes—it's very important not to overcook them or they'll lose their colour and go mushy. Drain them thoroughly and toss them in the dressing while they're still warm. When they're cool, toss in the finely chopped spring onion, the bacon and the chopped herbs. Serve the salad on some crisp lettuce leaves.

Salad Niçoise

(serves 4–6 people)

This is a favourite summer lunch dish in our house, served with *Hot herb and garlic loaf* (see page 600), but it also makes a nice refreshing and light first course.

1 lettuce
4 oz cooked new potatoes, sliced (110 g)
4 oz cooked French beans (110 g)
Half a small young cucumber, peeled and cut in smallish chunks
12 oz firm ripe tomatoes, skinned, de-seeded and quartered (350 g)
2 oz black olives (50 g)
2 hard-boiled eggs, peeled and quartered
1 × 7 oz tin tuna fish, well drained (200 g)
1 tablespoon finely chopped onion, or spring onions
1 tablespoon fresh chopped parsley
1 × 1¾ oz tin anchovy fillets, well drained (45 g)
Vinaigrette dressing with garlic and herbs (see page 576)—you won't need the full quantity of vinaigrette

First arrange lettuce leaves around the base of a large salad bowl and sprinkle on a little vinaigrette dressing. Then arrange the tomatoes and cucumber in layers with a little more dressing, then add the onion, slices of potatoes and French beans. Now place the quartered hard-boiled eggs on top with the tuna fish, which should be broken up into chunky flakes. Finally decorate the salad with the strips of anchovy fillet, making a latticed effect (or whatever you like), then sprinkle on the black olives, the fresh chopped parsley and the rest of the dressing. Serve as soon as possible.

Barbecues
and picnics

Including recipes for:
American hamburgers
Cevapcici
Anchoiade
Hot herb and garlic loaf
Italian stuffed aubergines
Mustard glazed lamb cutlets
Lamb kebabs
Pork spare ribs in barbecue sauce
Scotch eggs with fresh herbs
Bacon and egg pie
Spanish tortilla
Meat loaf
Banana and walnut loaf
Honey and spice cake

Eating out of doors is a bit of a hit-and-miss affair in this country for obvious reasons (such as getting only one week of sunshine in any one summer, for instance). If that sounds tongue in cheek, it's meant to because I feel the whole subject of outdoor eating in Britain should be approached with a sense of humour and with a certain flexibility.

Not that I'm a pessimist. Each spring I look at patio furniture in glossy magazines, and I dream dreams. These include candle-lit geraniums, the sizzling of charcoal-cooked food, the tinkle of ice-filled glasses, and all the rest. Such dreams never include the Suffolk winds that blow the smoke back in the direction of the guests, their eyes getting steadily redder, their coughs louder. Nor do they include what to do with fifty sausages (that fitted so well on the barbecue) having to go eight at a time under the grill in the kitchen because it's pouring! Even the most enthusiastic books on barbecues finish up with realistic advice, including among the recommended accessories, bug-repellant sprays and burn lotions.

As picnickers, too, we display the same kind of grim, resolute determination. In French films picnics are all about rivers and willows and punts, or fields of red poppies and buzzing bees. In Britain the hot tarmac of the zoo car-park will do, or a patch of grass with four lanes of traffic on either side. I have even seen a man and his wife, in a remote part of the Lake District, clad in sou'westers eating their lunch with plates perched on the car bonnet as the rain bucketed down! We all have our funny picnic stories, I'm sure. Nevertheless eating outdoors *is* fun and, if only to avoid eating in those motorway cafés, picnics are necessary.

Eating al fresco

The number one requirement for food in the open air is that it should have lots of gutsy flavour. Delicate, subtle dishes can easily lose their identity outside. Simple food—and lots of it—is the best, I've found: even the humble British banger is quite transformed with a smoky, crispy barbecued skin. Remember, too, that appetites mysteriously increase out of doors and people can eat more if the food is simple than if it's very rich.

Barbecues

If you're planning to improvise your own barbecue—or at the other end of the scale have ambitions for a built-in garden barbecue—then you should refer to one of several specialised books on the subject. For those of us in the middle who are content with a ready-made barbecue, however, there is a wide range of equipment and accessories to suit every taste and occasion. Basically there are only two kinds of barbecue: the brazier-type with a shallow bowl, where the air flows *over* the burning charcoal, and the grill-type with built-in air vents, where the air flows up and through the charcoal. All manner of attachments can be bought—hoods, spits, windshields, warming ovens—but none of these affect the basic operation.

Charcoal This is the commonest form of fuel, and comes either in pre-formed briquets (which are more efficient) or as lumpwood (which is cheaper). Hardwood can be used for large barbecues, but is quite impractical for the normal commercial makes.

Laying the fire On the brazier type of barbecue I think it is a good idea to line the bowl first with a sheet of aluminium foil (shiny side upwards), which will help to reflect the heat. Then lay a fire-bed of medium-sized gravel all over the base, so the air can circulate round the charcoal and help it to 'breathe'. Cover the fire-bed with a generous layer of charcoal, making sure it covers the whole area rather than just the centre and is not packed too tightly.

Lighting-up At home we use methylated spirit to get the charcoal alight—but it needs to be done with care. Sprinkle some all over the charcoal, then *wait* for a few minutes for it to get absorbed. Fire-lighters (broken up into smaller pieces and scattered among the charcoal) can be used, but don't start cooking until all the pieces are completely burned out, or the smoke will include some unpleasant fumes. In any case it is pointless to start cooking before the charcoal is properly and evenly alight, and that can take anything from 20–30 minutes. At night you can easily tell because the charcoal will glow pink: during the day the pieces will start to turn white.

Cooking on charcoal Try to set your barbecue where it will get a sufficient draught but is not directly in the wind. Most barbecues have a grill that can be adjusted to different heights above the fire, which will control the speed of cooking, but sooner or later fat from the food will drop onto the coals and ignite them into a fire. So have a jug of water handy and sprinkle a little onto the fire with your hands—just enough to douse the flame, but not to stop the coals burning.

For that extra smoky flavour you can add small chips of aromatic wood to the fire (such as hickory or apple-wood), but these chips should be well soaked in water before use, unless you buy specially prepared packets of 'smoke chips'. Fresh herbs, such as rosemary, also add an interesting flavour to the smoke: these should be sprinkled on the fire towards the end of the cooking.

Equipment Experience has taught me that implements with very long handles are what are called for in tending barbecue food! Long-handled tongs and fork (for turning the food) will keep your hands a safe distance from the heat and a pair of oven gloves will give added protection. For kebabs, thread the meat, etc onto *flat* skewers rather than round ones (which tend to turn themselves without turning the meat).

American hamburgers
(serves 2 people)

In this country the word hamburger conjures up all sorts of dubious connotations of frozen and packaged discs of meat and greasy griddles. The real hamburger is something else: 100% pure ground beef cooked, if possible, over charcoal to give it a charred, smoky crispness at the edges with a juicy medium-rare centre. All it needs then is a jacket potato brimming with soured cream and chives, and a selection of relishes and ketchup. This recipe will make 4 hamburgers to serve in buns, or two half-pounders (which may need a few more minutes cooking, depending on how you like them).

1 lb chuck steak, about 80 % lean meat and 20 % fat (450 g)
2 level teaspoons salt
Coarsely ground black pepper
A little oil

To prepare the meat you can either pass it through the fine blade of the mincer twice (which tenderises it), ask the butcher to do it for you, or you can grind the meat finely in a food processor.

To make the hamburgers, place the meat in a bowl and sprinkle in the salt and a good seasoning of coarsely ground black pepper.

Mix this in thoroughly, then divide the mixture into four portions. Take each portion in your hands and shape it into a ball, then place the ball on a flat surface and press to flatten it into a hamburger shape about ¾ inch (2 cm) thick.

Now brush each hamburger with very little oil and grill under a pre-heated grill set to high, or over hot charcoal, giving them 4–6 minutes on each side depending on how you like them. Serve in bap rolls (toasted on cut side only), and spread with slivers of raw or fried onion, relish and tomato ketchup.

Cevapcici (Yugoslav kebabs)

(serves 3–4 people)

These are delicious little minced sausages threaded onto skewers.

8 oz chuck steak (225 g)
8 oz lean belly pork or spare rib (225 g)
2 cloves garlic, crushed
1 teaspoon paprika
1 tablespoon finely chopped mint
Cayenne pepper
Salt and freshly-milled black pepper

For the sauce:
Approximately 4 inches (10 cm) cucumber, chopped into small cubes
5 fl oz natural yoghurt (150 ml)
2 teaspoons fresh chopped mint
1 clove garlic, crushed
Salt and freshly-milled black pepper

First the meats should be put through the finest blade of the mincer or chopped finely in a food processor. Then place them in a mixing bowl along with the garlic, paprika, a pinch of cayenne and a good seasoning of salt and pepper. Stir in the chopped mint and mix thoroughly to amalgamate everything. If possible, leave the mixture in a cool place for a while to allow the flavours to develop, then mould the mixture into about 9 little sausage shapes, about 2 inches (5 cm) in length. Thread these onto skewers—the flat kind are best—and cook over hot charcoal or under a pre-heated grill for 10–20 minutes, turning them frequently.

Serve them with a yoghurt sauce, made by simply combining all the sauce ingredients in a bowl.

Anchoïade

(serves 3–4 people)

This is a delicious snack to serve out of doors, either as a first course at a barbecue or for lunch with some 'salady' things to go with it. If it pours with rain, it can double up as a TV snack!

1 × 1¾ oz tin anchovy fillets in oil (45 g)
1 large or 2 small cloves garlic, crushed
8 black olives
1 small onion, finely chopped
A few drops of wine vinegar
1 tablespoon chopped parsley
1 ripe tomato, skinned and chopped
2 heaped teaspoons tomato purée
1 rounded teaspoon dried oregano or 2 teaspoons fresh chopped marjoram
8 × 1 inch (2·5 cm) thick slices of (day-old) French bread cut diagonally
Some olive oil
Freshly-milled black pepper
Extra chopped parsley for garnishing

Begin by pounding the anchovies (with their oil) to a pulp, either using a pestle and mortar or a basin and the end of a rolling-pin. Then pit the olives, chop their flesh up finely and add this to the anchovy mixture along with the chopped onion, tomato and a few drops of wine vinegar. Stir thoroughly, then add the crushed garlic, tomato purée, oregano, parsley and some freshly-milled pepper, and stir again.

Now lightly toast the French bread slices on one side only, then spread the mixture on the untoasted side. All this can be done in advance. Then to finish off, pour a few drops of oil over each slice, place them under a pre-heated medium grill for 5 minutes to heat through, and sprinkle with chopped parsley before serving.

Hot herb and garlic loaf

This is perfect for a barbecue or party when lots of salads are being served.

1 French stick loaf
3 oz butter, room temperature (75 g)
2 cloves garlic, crushed

2 tablespoons fresh chopped herbs (parsley and chives with a little tarragon and thyme if available) or 1½ teaspoons dried mixed herbs

Pre-heat the oven to gas mark 6, 400°F (200°C)

First mix the butter, garlic and herbs together. Using a sharp knife, make diagonal incisions along the loaf, as if you were slicing it—but not slicing right through. The loaf should stay joined at the base. Now spread each slice with butter on both sides (it's easiest to do this with your hands) and spread any remaining herb butter along the top and sides of the loaf. Wrap the loaf in foil and bake it in the oven for about 10–15 minutes, and serve hot.

Italian stuffed aubergines

(serves 3–6 people)

These are good to serve as a first course at a barbecue for six people or for lunch in the garden on a hot day for three people with a salad and cold drinks.

3 medium aubergines
1 onion, chopped
2 tablespoons olive oil
1 large clove garlic, crushed
About 6 oz Italian Mozzarella cheese (175 g)—or, failing that, Gouda cheese cut in thin slices
6 drained anchovy fillets, chopped
1½ tablespoons drained capers, chopped a little
3 largish tomatoes
2 teaspoons fresh chopped basil (or 1 teaspoon of dried basil)
A little additional oil
Salt and freshly-milled black pepper

Trim the green stalks from the aubergines and slice them in half lengthwise. If you have a grapefruit knife use that, or otherwise a teaspoon, to get out the pulpy centres of the aubergines leaving a shell not less than ¼ inch (½ cm) thick. Sprinkle the shells liberally with salt and leave upside down to drain for 45 minutes. Meanwhile chop the pulp.

Now heat the oil in a saucepan and gently fry the onion until softened. Stir in the chopped pulp, crushed garlic and half the basil. Season with salt and pepper and cook over a low heat for about 10 minutes, stirring now and then.

Next wipe the aubergine shells with kitchen paper and arrange them in a small oiled roasting tin or baking dish. Spoon the onion/pulp mixture into the shells, then arrange 2 slices of cheese on top of each aubergine half and sprinkle with the chopped capers and anchovies. Slice the tomatoes and arrange 4–5 slices on each aubergine. Finally sprinkle with the remaining basil and dribble a little more olive oil over each. Season and bake (uncovered) at gas mark 4, 350°F (180°C) in the top of the oven for 40 minutes.

Mustard glazed lamb cutlets

(serves 4 people)

These are best of all barbecued, but still taste very good grilled and they provide a special supper very quickly.

8 lamb cutlets
2 tablespoons made-up mustard (English or Dijon)
3 rounded tablespoons demerara sugar
Salt and freshly-milled black pepper

Pre-heat the grill to a high setting

Wipe the cutlets first with some absorbent kitchen paper to dry them, season them with salt and pepper, then spread both sides of each cutlet with mustard. Now dip them in the sugar, making sure they get an even coating, and grill them for about 5 minutes on each side—or more or less, depending on their thickness.

Lamb kebabs

(serves 4–6 people)

These are perhaps the nicest barbecue food of all but, if the weather is against you, fear not, they're almost as good when grilled indoors.

1½ lb fillet end of leg of lamb, or pieces from a boned-out shoulder (700 g)
6 tablespoons olive oil
1 medium-sized onion

2 large lemons
2 teaspoons dried oregano
6 small bayleaves
1 small green or red pepper, de-seeded
4 small tomatoes
2 cloves garlic, crushed
12 small mushrooms
Salt and freshly-milled black pepper

Start by preparing the meat: cut it into small bite-sized pieces (leaving some of the fat on the cubes as this helps to keep them juicy). Place the meat in a bowl, and then season it with salt and freshly-milled black pepper. Now add the bayleaves (snipped in half), crushed garlic and the oregano. Peel the onion and cut it into quarters, then separate the quarters into layers and add these to the meat together with the green or red pepper cut into ½ inch (1 cm) pieces.

Pour over the juice of one lemon, followed by the olive oil, and leave the meat to marinade (covered with a cloth) for several hours or overnight, stirring the ingredients and turning the meat cubes over now and then.

When you are ready to grill the kebabs, get your charcoal hot (or pre-heat your grill), then take a skewer—preferably a flattened one rather than a twisted or round one—and start by threading one mushroom and half a tomato (rounded end towards the handle of the skewer), then alternate a piece of meat, half a bayleaf, a piece of onion and a piece of pepper.

When everything is threaded onto the skewers, finish off with the other half of the tomato and the other mushroom. Push gently at both ends, because it's important everything be packed together as tightly as possible. Grill the kebabs, basting them from time to time with the oil marinade and turning them over. They'll take about 15–20 minutes to be charred nicely on the outside and pink and juicy within. Serve with the other lemon cut into quarters.

Pork spare ribs in barbecue sauce

(serves 4 people)

Pork spare ribs (the actual rib bones) or lean pork slices are both good coated and flavoured with a barbecue sauce.

12 spare ribs

For the sauce:
3 tablespoons dry white wine or dry cider
6 tablespoons soy sauce
1 clove garlic
1 rounded tablespoon tomato purée
1 teaspoon English mustard powder
1 level tablespoon soft brown sugar
A few drops of tabasco sauce
Freshly-milled black pepper

First crush the garlic in a bowl, and pour in the wine (or cider) and soy sauce. Then stir in the tomato purée, followed by the mustard powder and sugar. Next add a few drops of tabasco, then give it all a good stir and season with pepper—no salt is needed because soy sauce is quite salty.

Leave the sauce a few moments for the flavours to develop, then when the meat is ready to be cooked, brush each side generously with the barbecue sauce.

Grill or barbecue the meat for about 15 minutes on each side, basting now and then with the extra sauce.

Picnics and food for travelling

When it comes to picnics nothing will budge me an inch from my keep-it-simple philosophy. In Edwardian days it was all very well, when butler, maid, bar and fully-equipped hamper could be transplanted into the country. And if you're very rich, I suppose you can still pick up a Henley or an Ascot Hamper from one of the smart London food establishments (though whether the contents will warrant the price is debatable). For less grand affairs I feel many people go wrong by trying to transport the sort of meal they would eat at home: it just doesn't taste the same on squashy paper plates with plastic knives and forks, that come in sizes fit only for 4-year-olds.

Rough outdoor living demands rough outdoor food. Some of the nicest picnics I've had have been in Italy—crusty bread, chunks of salami, ripe plum tomatoes, cheese, olives, pickled pimentoes, peaches and huge black cherries, and of course quantities of something Italian to drink. All we had to pack on these occasions was pepper and salt, an insulated dish for butter, knives, plates and glasses. No cooking was involved, you will note. Even in this country you can approximate this kind of ready-made picnic by stopping at a chain-store with a good food department and buying bread, pork pies, salads in tubs, good fruit and a cake.

However if you're not pushed for time and want to plan and prepare a picnic, all the recipes in this section will serve you well out of doors or, if there's a last minute change of weather, inside.

Equipment

Our picnic equipment, such as it is, is not very elegant: I have found that a few old china plates and mugs, and odd knives and forks, are infinitely preferable to anything in the plastic line. We also have some thick chunky glasses which may not look very sophisticated but are far nicer—especially if you're drinking wine—than paper cups. In fact the only 'special' equipment I have is a thermos flask and a wide thermos jug (for soup in cold weather), an insulated butter dish (if you put very cold butter in it, it keeps cool all day), and an insulated bag with a little freezer pad (which also keep things cool when it is frozen and placed inside). Oh, and two other important items: a peppermill and a corkscrew!

To keep things like cakes and rolls fresh, I think the best thing is to wrap them first in greaseproof paper, then in foil and place them in plastic bags. Polythene boxes are all right, but in our house by the time we've found the right lid to fit the right box, there's no time for a picnic.

Picnic foods

French bread This is excellent for picnics, sliced diagonally, split, buttered and filled with slices of strong Cheddar cheese and sliced raw onion, then sandwiched together again.

Bap rolls These are delicious filled with the following mixture (for 6 people): mash 6 boiled eggs while they're still warm with a good knob of butter, 4 teaspoons mayonnaise, salt and pepper. Stir in 2 heaped tablespoons of fresh snipped chives.

Crusty rolls Buy garlic sausage or salami in one piece, so that you can slice it more thickly. Fill the rolls with this plus some thin slices of (drained) dill pickled cucumbers.

Garlic butter If you mash a clove of garlic into 8 oz (225 g) butter along with 2 tablespoons of chopped parsley, then chill it all well and place in an insulated butter dish, this will be lovely to spread on French bread or rolls.

Rice salad This is a handy salad to take on a picnic, because it is dressed beforehand (see page 586). I pack it in individual foil containers with lids, and find it travels very well.

Crunchy things are nice at picnics—for instance, radishes and crisp spring onions. Firm tomatoes are a good idea, but it goes without saying that they should be taken whole: never slice them or put them in sandwiches, they're too soggy (and that goes for cucumbers too). Some of my own favourite picnic recipes are included in this chapter but, of course, earlier parts of the Cookery Course also contain several that are suitable for travelling.

Let me remind you of some. *Boeuf en croûte* (Part One, page 92) is rather extravagant perhaps, but left to cool, then cut in slices, it's a super idea for a special picnic. *Shoulder of lamb with rice and kidney stuffing* (Part One, page 141) also cuts very well into thick slices. *Sausage rolls* (Part One, page 91) are picnic perennials that never fail. *Quick wholewheat pizza* (Part One, page 66), cut into sections and wrapped carefully, tastes marvellous in the open air. *Mustard-and-herb coated chicken* (Part Two, page 401) need no plates or knives and forks, so are good for car journeys. *Cold chicken pie* (Part Two, page 405) should be taken in the tin it was cooked in, double wrapped, then cut when you arrive. *Date, apple and walnut loaf* (Part Two, page 272) is a nice moist cake with a crunchy crust.

Scotch eggs with fresh herbs

(makes 4)

Scotch eggs are marvellous for travellers or picnickers. Take some spring onions to go with them and, if you've got plates (paper or otherwise), take some chutney to 'dunk' the sausagemeat into.

4 hard-boiled eggs
8 oz sausagemeat (225 g)
2 spring onions, finely chopped
1 teaspoon fresh thyme, finely chopped
3 teaspoons chives, snipped
1 tablespoon parsley, finely chopped
Some toasted breadcrumbs
Seasoned plain flour
1 small egg, beaten
Salt and freshly-milled black pepper
Oil for frying

Hard-boil the eggs by covering them in cold water, bringing it to the boil, simmering gently for 9 minutes and cooling them under cold running water. Next mix the sausagemeat with the spring onions and herbs and season well. Then shell the cooled eggs and coat each one with some seasoned flour. Divide the sausagemeat into four portions and pat each piece out on a floured surface to a shape roughly 5 × 3 inches (13 cm × 7·5 cm). Now place an egg in the centre of each piece and carefully gather up the sausagemeat to completely cover the egg. Seal the joins well, and smooth and pat into shape all over. Next coat them one by one, first in beaten egg and then thoroughly and evenly in toasted breadcrumbs.

Now heat 1½ inches (4 cm) of oil in a deep frying pan up to a temperature of 350°–375°F (180°–190°C). (If you don't have a thermometer, you can easily test the temperature by frying a small cube of bread—if it turns golden brown within 1 minute the oil is hot enough.) Put the eggs into the oil and fry for 6–8 minutes turning frequently until they have turned a nice brown colour. Drain on crumpled greaseproof paper.

When they're absolutely cold, wrap in clingfilm and store in the lower part of the fridge.

Bacon and egg pie

(serves 4–6 people)

A home-made bacon and egg pie makes a very good and easily transportable picnic dish, I find. Alternatively, it's nice served warm after the 'picnic' if the weather wasn't up to scratch!

4 large eggs
6 rashers lean, streaky bacon
5 fl oz milk (150 ml)
Salt and freshly-milled black pepper

Shortcrust pastry made with:
6 oz plain flour (175 g)
3 oz lard (75 g)
Pinch of salt and pepper
Cold water (to mix)

Pre-heat the oven (and a baking sheet) to gas mark 6, 400°F (200°C)

An 8 inch (20 cm) flan tin, rimmed if
possible and 1½ inches (4 cm) deep.

Hard-boil three of the eggs—which I do by putting them in a
saucepan, covering them with cold water, bringing to the boil and
simmering gently for 9 minutes. Cool them quickly by running
cold water from the tap over them. Then, while they're cooling,
grill (or fry) the bacon gently until the fat begins to run, and make
up the shortcrust pastry. Now divide the pastry in half, using one
half to line the flan tin.

Peel and chop the hard-boiled eggs quite small, chop the bacon
fairly small too and arrange them both in the flan. Season with
freshly-milled pepper and a very little salt. Beat the remaining egg
together with the milk, then pour the mixture over the contents of
the pie. Roll out the rest of the pastry to form a lid, dampen the
edges and seal well all round, using any trimmings to decorate.
Make a small hole in the centre of the pastry, brush the top with
milk, then put on the baking sheet on a high shelf in the oven and
bake for 10 minutes. After that reduce the heat to gas mark 4,
350°F (180°C) and bake for a further 30 minutes.

Little Bacon and Egg Pies
Alternatively you can make individual pies in 2½ inch (6 cm) patty
tins, using 3 inch (7·5 cm) and 3½ inch (8 cm) cutters.

For 11–12 little pies you'll need: the quantity of pastry as above,
2 hard-boiled eggs, 4 rashers back bacon, 1 egg and 4 fl oz (100 ml)
milk beaten together.

Use the larger rounds of pastry to line the patty tins, divide
the chopped eggs and bacon between the pies, then pour in the
egg-and-milk mixture, and top with the smaller pastry rounds.
Brush the tops with any left-over egg-and-milk mixture, and bake
on a pre-heated baking sheet in the oven at gas mark 6, 400°F
(200°C) for 10 minutes, then reduce the heat to gas mark 5, 375°F
(190°C) and cook for a further 25 minutes.

Spanish tortilla

(serves 2–4 people)

This is an omelette which is just as nice
served cold as it is hot—and excellent
therefore for taking on a picnic, where
you can cut it up into wedges.

4 large eggs
2 medium-sized potatoes, peeled and diced small
1 small green pepper, de-seeded and chopped
1 medium onion, chopped
2 oz piece Spanish chorizo sausage (or similar), cut into small dice (50 g)
3 tablespoons olive oil
Salt and freshly-milled black pepper

Begin by heating 2 tablespoons of the oil in a frying pan, add the potatoes and cook them for 8–10 minutes (stirring them from time to time) until they're evenly browned. Then add the onion, pepper and sausage. Give them all a good stir and carry on cooking for another 6–8 minutes.

Now beat the eggs and season them well with salt and pepper, and pour them into the frying pan over the vegetable mixture. Cook over a medium heat for 3 minutes or so, drawing the cooked egg into the centre of the pan with a palette knife and letting the liquid egg run into the gaps. When the omelette is firm—but still slightly moist—turn it upside down onto a plate. Then heat the remaining tablespoon of oil in the pan and slide the omelette back into the pan (other side up). Cook it for a further 3 minutes. You can of course serve this straightaway; otherwise leave to get cold, cover and keep in a cool place until needed.

Meat loaf
(serves 6–8 people)

This is a good idea for a picnic as, once cold, it can be cut into firm slices. However, it's also very good served hot with a fresh tomato sauce.

1 lb lean minced beef (450 g)—from a reliable butcher
8 oz minced pork, or pork sausagemeat (225 g)
2 medium-sized onions, minced
1 small green pepper, finely chopped
1 dessertspoon tomato purée
1 fat clove garlic, crushed
1 level teaspoon dried mixed herbs

2 tablespoons fresh chopped parsley
2 slices white bread from a large loaf
3 tablespoons milk
1 egg, beaten
Salt and freshly-milled black pepper

Pre-heat the oven to gas mark 5, 375°F (190°C)

A 2 lb loaf tin (900 g)

Put the minced beef in a large mixing bowl with the pork, onion, chopped pepper, tomato purée and garlic and give everything a thorough mixing, seasoning well with salt and freshly-milled pepper. Cut the crusts off the bread, soak it in the milk, then squeeze the excess milk out of it and add it to the rest of the ingredients, along with the mixed herbs and parsley. Now give the mixture another thorough mixing, and finally stir in the beaten egg to bind it all together.

Press the mixture into a 2 lb (900 g) loaf tin, spreading evenly, then bake it in the oven for 1¼ hours. When it's cooked it will have shrunk and begun to come away from the sides of the tin. Allow it to get cold in the tin, wrap it in a double sheet of foil and take it to the picnic wrapped in a cloth or in an oblong plastic box.

Note: meat loaf is delicious served cold with pickles and salad. It also goes very well sliced and put into sandwiches or rolls.

All-in-one banana and walnut loaf

This is an extremely easy loaf cake, ideal for picnics as it has a good pronounced flavour.

3 oz soft margarine (75 g)
4 oz caster sugar (110 g)
1 large egg, beaten
The grated rind of 1 orange
The grated rind of 1 lemon
8 oz plain flour (225 g)
2 level teaspoons baking powder
4 medium bananas, peeled
2 oz walnuts (50 g), roughly chopped

Pre-heat the oven to gas mark 4, 350°F (180°C)

A loaf tin, base measuring $3\frac{1}{2} \times 7\frac{1}{2}$ inches (8·5 × 19 cm), greased, with the base lined with greaseproof paper also greased

Start off by placing the margarine, sugar and the beaten egg in a large mixing bowl, then sift in the flour and baking powder. In another bowl slice the bananas and mash them to a pulp with a fork. Now, use an electric mixer to whisk the sugar, fat and flour together until they are thoroughly combined—don't worry if the mixture looks rather dry at this stage. Next add the orange and lemon rinds, followed by the mashed bananas and chopped walnuts, and whisk again thoroughly. Then transfer the mixture to the prepared tin and level the top off.

Bake on the centre shelf of the oven for 50–55 minutes, until the loaf is golden, well-risen and springs back when pressed with a finger. Leave to cool in the tin for 10 minutes, then loosen around the edges and turn out onto a wire cooling tray to finish cooling. This cake is nice sliced and spread with butter.

Honey and spice cake

This cake has a tangy, citrus flavour—perfect for the open air. Because it has a lemon icing, it is best transported in a polythene box.

8 oz plain flour (225 g)
4 oz butter (110 g)
3 oz caster sugar (75 g)
1 level teaspoon ground ginger
1 level teaspoon ground cinnamon
$\frac{1}{4}$ teaspoon ground cloves
The finely grated zest of 1 small orange
The finely grated zest of 1 small lemon
1 large egg, beaten
3 oz clear, runny honey (75 g)
1 level teaspoon bicarbonate of soda
2 oz finely chopped mixed candied peel (50 g)

For the icing:

---

4 oz sifted icing sugar (110 g)

1½ tablespoons lemon juice

---

2 tablespoons warm water

To decorate:

---

6 pieces crystallised ginger, chopped

Pre-heat the oven to gas mark 3,
325°F (170°C)

One 7 inch (18 cm) square tin, lightly
buttered

First of all weigh a cup or small basin on the scales then weigh 3 oz
(75 g) of honey into it. Now place the basin into a saucepan
containing barely simmering water and warm the honey a little
but be careful, it mustn't be too hot, just warm. Next sift the flour
and spices into a large mixing bowl, then add the sugar and the
orange and lemon zest. Now add the butter in small pieces, then
rub it lightly into the flour, using your fingertips, until the mixture
becomes crumbly. Next, lightly mix in the beaten egg, using a
large fork, followed by the warm honey. Then in a small basin, mix
the bicarbonate of soda with 3 tablespoons of cold water, stir until
dissolved, then add it to the cake mixture and beat, quite hard,
until the mixture is smooth and soft. Then, finally, stir in the
mixed peel and spoon the mixture into the prepared tin, spreading
it out evenly. Bake the cake just above the centre of the oven for
about 30 minutes or until well risen and springy to the touch. Cool
it for about 10 minutes, then turn it out onto a wire rack to get
quite cold.

Meanwhile prepare the icing by sifting the icing sugar into a bowl,
then add 2 tablespoons of warm water along with the lemon juice
and mix to a thin consistency that will coat the back of a spoon. If
you don't think it's thin enough add a little more water. Now place
the cake on a wire rack, with a large plate underneath, and pour
the icing all over, letting it run down and coat the sides a bit. Then
decorate the top with the chopped ginger and store in an airtight
tin until needed.

Herbs

Writing in the 16th century the East Anglian farmer Thomas Tusser listed over fifty herbs that he considered *essential* in every kitchen garden, and at one time—in fact until just over 200 years ago—London's Leadenhall had its very own herb market. The fact that it closed down is probably a sad reflection on the decline of the use of herbs in English cooking. And not just cooking, for every cook book right up to the last century contained its own batch of herbal healing remedies for a whole litany of ailments, from toothache to gout!

I suppose the decline of herbs ran parallel to the decline of our cooking, at the time the industrial revolution enticed people off the land. But now, two centuries later, I think nature is luring us back from our modern technology to consider what the earth gives— fresh natural foods and fresh natural flavours, and not least the enormous variety of fragrant and fresh-tasting herbs. Living in the country I am fortunate enough to have room for a fairly large herb garden, but even in the cities more and more people have recently set up their window boxes or growbags to plant a few fresh herbs to enliven their cooking.

Even if that isn't possible, fresh herbs can now be purchased in some shops and supermarkets. There are quite a number of herb farms which send them out by post (which is a slightly extravagant way of acquiring them, since it involves ever-increasing postal charges). But if we keep on pestering those greengrocers who don't yet stock a decent range of fresh herbs, we will eventually get a steadier and more reliable supply of them.

Storing herbs

For those who have to buy fresh cut herbs, do *not* store them stuck in a jar of water on a window sill. Sunlight ruins cut herbs, so tie them loosely but securely in polythene bags and park them in the lowest part of the refrigerator (i.e. a vegetable drawer). In this way I have kept cut chives, tarragon and chervil for up to a week, mint for a fortnight, and thyme, sage and rosemary even longer.

Freezing herbs

I have found that the best way to freeze them for my own use is actually to make herb butter (either of mixed herbs or individual ones, see Part One, page 163). A good way to do this is to press the butter into ice-cube trays, and slip the trays into polythene bags before putting back in the freezer. This makes it very convenient to use just one or two blocks for melting over steaks, fish or vegetables.

Chopping herbs

There are plenty of little gadgets on the market for chopping herbs, but none as good as a sharp knife and wooden chopping board. The trouble with many of these gadgets is that they squash—rather than chop—the herbs and make them mushy (they also require tedious and intricate cleaning afterwards!).

Ideally you need a good-sized cook's knife, with a 7 inch (18 cm) blade that is slightly curved. Arrange the herbs on the chopping board by spreading them out, then rest the blade of the knife horizontally on the board at the edge furthest away from you. Hold the pointed end between the finger and thumb of one hand to steady it, take the handle in your other hand, and make sharp cutting movements swinging the handle towards you as you chop—so that the blade swivels in a fan shape across the herbs, and back again. Your reward, I promise, will be a deliciously aromatic, herb-scented kitchen.

Chives are an exception as they are far easier snipped with kitchen scissors. I have also heard it said (and I pass it on to you) that basil should have its leaves torn rather than chopped: this apparently is the best way to retain all the fragrant oils.

Cooking with fresh herbs

In some recipes whole sprigs of herbs are added to the pot at the beginning of the cooking, so that their flavour can truly permeate the food, but this depends entirely on the nature of the dish and the herb itself. There are times (especially when making sauces or soups) when it is far better to add the herb at the very end, just before serving, so that none of the freshness or fragrance is lost. Examples of this would be chives in leek soup, parsley in parsley sauce, and basil in tomato sauce.

Dried herbs

For home drying of herbs I would point you in the direction of the book list at the end of this book, since this is something that requires care and expertise. However, commercially dried herbs are very useful in the kitchen at certain times of the year. Some cooks despise the use of dried herbs altogether—and I would agree that some herbs like chives, parsley and particularly mint, lose all their charm and flavour when dried. Nevertheless there are those that deserve their place in the kitchen, and in my notes on the varieties of herbs beginning on the next page I have indicated which these are.

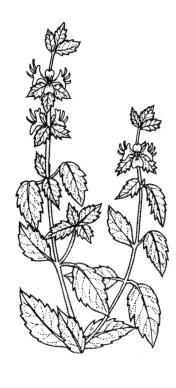

Basil

In my kitchen basil reigns supreme (appropriately enough, since its name is derived from the Greek word *basileus* for king!). It is used extensively in Italian and Provençal cooking, has a warm pungent scent and—to me—a taste of the sun. It is lack of sun that makes it difficult to grow here if we have a cold summer, yet I've always managed to grow some in a pot on my kitchen window-sill. Provided the white flowers are pinched off all the time, it goes on producing leaves right through until the end of October.

The fresh leaves are quite delicious, chopped and sprinkled over a tomato salad, or added to sauces and soups just before serving. Anything that has tomato in it will be improved with the addition of basil—the two have a great affinity. Dried basil has nowhere near the character and flavour of the fresh leaves—but dried basil is better than no basil at all, and it's fine in soups and sauces through the winter.

Bayleaves

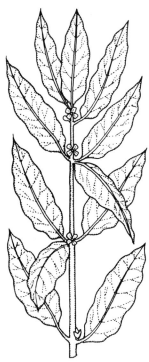

Bay trees, with their glossy green leaves, can be quite prolific. I have one about 2 feet (60 cm) high, which gives me all the bayleaves I need. Fresh bayleaves, however, can impart a slightly bitter flavour, so this is a herb which is far better used dried. To dry them is easy: just hang a branch in an airy spot and the leaves will dry in a couple of weeks.

They are used probably more than any other herb, to flavour stocks, sauces, casseroles and marinades. One unusual idea you might like to try is to place a bayleaf in about 2 inches (5 cm) of

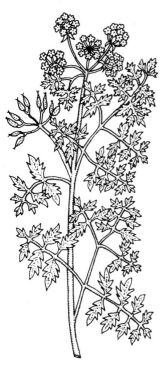

boiling water, add some salt, then sit a whole prepared cauliflower in the water to cook with the lid tightly closed. When it's tender (about 10 minutes), drain, melt some butter over the cauliflower, and sprinkle on a little nutmeg.

Chervil

This herb is used quite a lot in French cooking, but rather less in this country where we tend to prefer the more pungent flavour of parsley. Chervil in fact has a more subtle, delicate flavour, and it is quite easy to grow. Along with a few chives and chopped tarragon, it's delicious in an *Omelette aux fines herbes* (Part One, page 29). It can be used in sauces too, but (like parsley) should be added at the last moment if it is to make any sort of impression. Chervil is not good dried.

Chives

I wouldn't be without my chives—a very easily grown perennial that adds interest to a whole variety of dishes from early April right through to October. Although a member of the onion family, chives have a sweet flavour entirely their own. A catalogue of how to use them would be endless: they turn up in very many dishes all through the Cookery Course, but one of my favourite ways of serving them is to add a couple of heaped tablespoons to 5 fl oz (150 ml) of soured cream, and to pour this over halved jacket potatoes.

Don't chop chives—keep them in bunches and use scissors to snip them in small pieces. They can be deep-frozen for the winter by placing them in a sieve, pouring boiling water over to blanch them, then cooling them under a cold

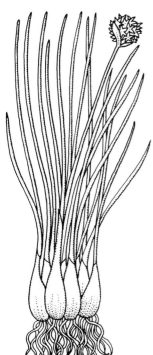

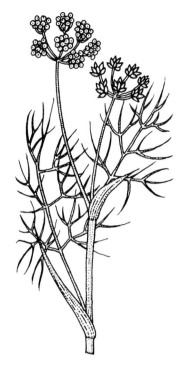

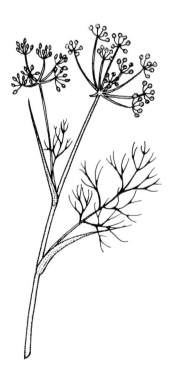

tap. Dry them as thoroughly as possible and freeze in sealed polythene bags.

Dried chives don't work at all, but if you can get hold of a clump (or seeds) of Welsh onion, scallion or green onion (which all look like spring onion tops) you'll find these go on all through the winter. Although they have a slightly stronger flavour, they're suitable for any recipe that calls for chives.

Dill

This herb is best-known for its use in commercially pickled cucumbers, where the leafy heads and the seeds are used. The seeds have to be planted annually, but grow very easily; the feathery leaves have a sharp, aromatic flavour. Chopped they are good in sauces for fish, or added to butter to melt over. Dill goes particularly well with soured cream dressings or sauces, and has a great affinity with cucumber: add 2 tablespoons chopped to *Cucumber sauce* (Part One, page 153), or try the recipe for cucumber cooked with dill on page 632. I find dried dill can be used successfully if you infuse the leaves in warm water for a few minutes, then drain and use as fresh.

Fennel

Garden fennel is a fern-like green herb with quite a pronounced aniseed flavour (just as strong as that of bulb fennel described in the Vegetable chapter, page 643). It's good in sauces or stuffing for fish. An interesting variation on the *Italian baked fish* recipe (Part One, page 107) is to add a dessertspoon of chopped fennel leaves to the tomato sauce before pouring it over the fish for baking.

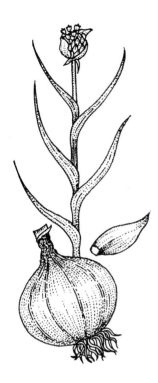

Garlic

I think of garlic (strictly a member of the onion family) as more of an essential seasoning—and as such it has been fully dealt with in Part One. I am often teased about my constant use of garlic, but remain unrepentant: you can, if you truly dislike it, always leave it out, but time and again I have heard from other cooks that garlic has often been added to dishes served to garlic-haters and they've been none the wiser! If like me you happen to love it, did you know it's very easy to grow? All you do is separate the cloves (individual sections) from the bulb, and plant them 2 inches (5 cm) deep and about 2 inches (5 cm) apart in early spring. Then in August you can harvest your own crop: firm, juicy and tasting so much better than the imported ones.

One way to crush garlic—a question I'm asked all the time—is to place the clove on a board, set the flat side of a small knife on top and press with your thumb until you have squashed it to a pulp. You could invest in a proper garlic crusher, though these are tiresome things to clean. Probably the best way is with a pestle and mortar: add a little salt as this helps to reduce the garlic to a smooth paste. And one tip for peeling garlic—place the unpeeled clove on a flat surface and simply press it with your thumb. This breaks the skin all over, and it peels away very easily.

Lovage

This is a herb that hardly ever crops up in recipes, yet proliferates in (almost dominates) herb gardens. It has a strong flavour which I can only describe

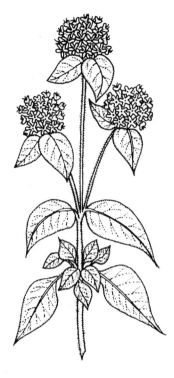

as a sort of pungent, aromatic celery. It's worth growing to make into a lovely green, summery soup, or you can use the leaves in stocks, sauces or anything else that requires a little celery flavour.

Marjoram

There are three different varieties of this plant. Pot marjoram is a perennial herb which is inclined to spread itself all over the space that is allocated to it. Sweet marjoram is a half-hearted perennial (because it won't survive a hard winter). And there is wild marjoram, which in Greece is called rigani or oregano. I grow the first type, because I'm not organised enough to sow a new batch each year. I use it, along with other herbs, for herb butters, herb omelettes and herb-flavoured dressings for salads. Fresh pot marjoram can be used for any recipe that calls for oregano, but for winter use I would strongly recommend dried oregano.

Mint

Mint comes in a whole range of varieties that can be used for cooking, and when I first started a herb garden I found myself the proud owner of several kinds. However I gradually came to realise that spearmint was the one I used most, and now grow only that. This is the one used for mint sauce, and for cooking new potatoes. When it's being chopped the kitchen is filled with the most fragrant aroma; and a couple of sprigs added to boiling new potatoes will also permeate the room with an appetising smell too. In the summer it is, like chives, a herb I use frequently, and it's included in several recipes that follow.

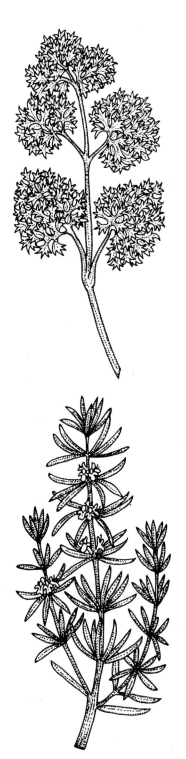

One unusual application I discovered in the Amalfi area of Italy is to place fresh mint leaves in the belly of fish before baking, grilling or frying them.

One word of warning about mint: never use it dried—it loses all its flavour and becomes very musty and lifeless.

Parsley

What needs to be said about the most universal and widely-used herb of all? No garden or window-box should be without it. The leaves can be used to flavour and enliven the appearance of many, many dishes. The stalks may be added to stocks, while sprigs of parsley are the most ubiquitous garnish of the lot. To keep a good supply going, it's best to sow some seeds in late spring and again at the end of summer, as the plant is a biennial.

Rosemary

The ancient Greeks said that rosemary was good for the brain—a theory that persisted through the centuries (so we find Ophelia presenting it to Hamlet 'for remembrance'). Be that as it may, the Italians love its strong spicy flavour in the kitchen, and make no excuses for using it. The French are more subtle with it, but there are many countries that hardly use it at all.

There are those who say that rosemary can be unpleasant if it gets stuck between the teeth—but this doesn't happen if the needle-like leaves are stripped from their stems and then chopped before using. It has a strong affinity with both pork and lamb, and can be chopped and sprinkled over joints and chops before baking (you'll

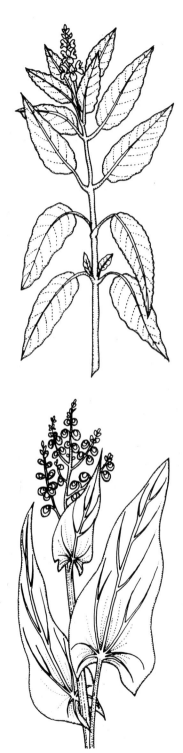

find you can make a lovely rosemary-flavoured sauce with the juices left in the tin with some stock and a little red or white wine).

Rosemary grows very easily into a sturdy bush, and can be used fresh all through the winter. Dried rosemary is all right, but I would recommend that it be chopped as finely as possible since it's much more spiky when dried.

Sage

Sage has always been one of the great healing herbs: its name comes from the Latin *salvere* (to save). Its culinary use is largely despised by the French, but much favoured by the British and Italians. It is a very strongly-flavoured herb, so has to be used with caution. Delicious in stuffings for all poultry and pork (see the recipe on page 632), and especially good in pork sausages.

It is easy to grow, though as with mint, there are many varieties. I grow the broad leaf sage. This is a herb that does dry well, without losing much flavour at all.

Sorrel

Much-loved and used for sauces and soups in France, but not so widely known here. Yet it's easy to grow and well worth including in a herb garden. It has leaves similar in appearance to spinach, and indeed tastes like a sharper version of spinach. Because of this sharpness very little of it is needed—a couple of handfuls, about 1½ oz (40 g) is enough to make a delicious soup.

Tarragon

If the king of herbs is basil, then I would like to nominate tarragon as the queen. It's a sophisticated herb, highly prized in French cooking and an essential ingredient in their famous *Béarnaise sauce* (see Part One, page 153). It goes well in veal and poultry dishes, and is often included in mixed herb dishes. It is, however, a strongly flavoured herb, so always be sparing with it. A sprig or two preserved in some white wine vinegar will help to give a subtle flavour of tarragon to salad dressings all through the winter.

You can only grow it from cuttings, and if you buy a plant (one will be enough) do make sure the label says it's French tarragon. There is a Russian variety which grows up to 5 feet (1·5 m) high, but has nowhere near the flavour of the French. Dried tarragon is useful—if you steep it in warm water for a minute or two before using.

Thyme

A bush of garden thyme will be a good friend to any cook, as it provides fresh leaves all the year round. It has a really strong, warm resinous flavour, and needs to be used sparingly if it is not to overpower other tastes. A teaspoonful of chopped thyme added to a salad dressing is a good idea, and I use little branches of thyme in my stocks and casseroles—and always add some to beef stews. You'll find it in many recipes in the Cookery Course, and as it is a herb that dries well, it's useful for flat dwellers and non-gardeners.

Green herb soup

(serves 4–5 people)

This soup adapts to any combination of fresh herbs—mint, sage, lovage, thyme, rosemary, sorrel or any others that are available.

1 oz butter (25 g)
6 thick spring onions (and their green tops), thinly sliced
6 oz potatoes, scraped and cubed (175 g)
5 oz outside lettuce leaves, or spinach leaves, de-stalked and shredded (150 g)
2 rounded tablespoons chopped fresh herbs
15 fl oz light stock (425 ml)
5 fl oz single cream (150 ml)
A generous squeeze of lemon juice
Salt and freshly-milled black pepper

Melt the butter in a medium-sized pan, and stir in the thinly sliced spring onions and the cubed potatoes. Stir and cook over a gentle heat so the vegetables soften gently without browning.

Now stir in the shredded lettuce. Get it all nicely coated with butter. Then add the stock, bring to simmering point, cover and cook gently for about 10 minutes or just long enough for the potatoes to soften.

Next pour the contents of the saucepan into a liquidiser. Add the chopped fresh herbs and the cream and blend until smooth. Return the purée to the pan and re-heat, tasting and flavouring with the lemon juice, salt and pepper. Serve piping hot with some fresh, crusty wholewheat bread.

Carrot and tarragon soup

(serves 4–6 people)

This is a delicious, summery soup, but it can be made in the winter with 2 finely chopped leeks instead of the lettuce leaves and some dried tarragon instead of fresh.

12 oz carrots (350 g)
The outside leaves of a lettuce (or 2 finely chopped leeks)
1 small onion

2 sprigs fresh tarragon, or $\frac{1}{4}$ teaspoon dried
1$\frac{1}{2}$ pints boiling water (850 ml)
2 oz butter (50 g)
3 tablespoons double cream
1 teaspoon sugar
Salt and freshly-milled black pepper

First wash and scrape the carrots and slice them thinly, then chop the onion and lettuce fairly small. In a thick-based saucepan gently melt the butter and soften the onion in it for a minute or two, then add the carrots and lettuce, stirring to get a good coating of butter. Now put a lid on and let the vegetables gently 'sweat' for 10 minutes. Next, strip the leaves from the tarragon, pop them in, then add the boiling water, the sugar and a seasoning of salt and pepper. When it returns to simmering point, put a lid on and simmer very gently for 25 minutes. Now either liquidise or sieve the soup, taste to check the seasoning and reheat gently, stirring in the cream just before serving.

Note: don't be tempted to use stock, as this detracts from the fresh flavour of the carrots.

Spring sauce for lamb

I always part company with mint sauce if it's made with malt vinegar which completely overpowers the flavour of lamb, but the following sauce—which my grandmother always served with lamb—is made with wine vinegar diluted with an equal quantity of water, so it's much milder.

2 tablespoons fresh chopped mint
2 spring onions very finely chopped
2 lettuce leaves finely shredded and chopped
3 tablespoons wine vinegar
3 tablespoons cold water

Simply combine all the above ingredients and place in a sauce-boat for everyone to help themselves. The quantities given will be enough for 6 people.

Pesto alla Genovese (fresh basil sauce)

(serves 3 people)

This is a sauce which, freshly made, will throw any pasta lover into transports of delight. The flavour of the fresh basil combined with olive oil and garlic is out of this world!

2 oz fresh basil leaves (50 g)
1 large clove garlic, crushed
1 tablespoon pine kernels
6 tablespoons olive oil
1 oz grated Parmesan cheese (25 g)
Salt

If you have a blender, then put the basil, garlic, pine kernels and olive oil together with some salt in the goblet and blend until you have a smooth purée. Then transfer the purée to a bowl and stir in the grated Parmesan.

If you don't have a blender, use a large pestle and mortar to pound the basil, garlic and pine kernels to a paste. Slowly add the salt and cheese followed by the very gradual addition of the oil until you obtain a smooth purée.

The above quantities will make enough sauce for serving with 12 oz (225 g) of pasta, which is sufficient for 3–4 people.

Fresh tomato sauce with basil

(serves 2–4 people)

This is one of the nicest sauces of all— it really tastes of summer. Serve it with absolutely anything that needs sauce— especially pasta.

12 oz red, ripe tomatoes, peeled and chopped (350 g)
1 small onion, finely chopped
1 clove garlic, crushed
1 teaspoon tomato purée
1 tablespoon fresh chopped basil or 1 teaspoon dried
2 tablespoons olive oil
Salt and freshly-milled black pepper

First peel the tomatoes by pouring boiling water over them, leave them for a minute or two, then put them in cold water, and slip the skins off. Now halve them, discard most of the seeds and chop the flesh quite small.

Then heat the oil in a thick-based saucepan, add the onion and garlic, and when they've softened add the tomatoes, tomato purée, the dried basil and seasoning. If you are using fresh basil, add it at the end. Stir well, then simmer gently for 15 minutes with the lid on, and for a further 10 or 15 minutes without the lid. This will allow some of the excess liquid to reduce, and concentrate the flavour. Taste to check the seasoning, then either sieve the mixture or blend it in a liquidiser—or if you like, serve it just as it is.

Green herb and rice salad

(serves 8 people)

This is an excellent way to serve rice, cold at a buffet party or warm with barbecue food.

Brown rice measured to the 12 fl oz (300 ml) level in a glass measuring jug
24 fl oz boiling water or stock (670 ml)—double the volume of rice
1 teaspoon salt
2 oz prepared spinach leaves (50 g)
8 spring onions including the green tops
2 heaped teaspoons chopped herbs (thyme, rosemary, sage, savory, marjoram, tarragon)
2 dessertspoons oil
The grated rind of half a lemon
For the dressing:
½ teaspoon black peppercorns
1 clove garlic
1 teaspoon rock salt
1 teaspoon mustard powder
1 tablespoon wine vinegar
5 tablespoons olive oil

Heat the two dessertspoons of oil in a pan, stir in the rice, then pour in the boiling water or stock. Add 1 teaspoon of salt, stir once and allow it to come back to the boil. Cover, then reduce the heat to give a bare simmer. Cook gently for 40–45 minutes or until all the liquid has been absorbed and the rice is just tender.

Next chop up the spinach leaves and spring onions very finely, and fork into the rice along with the herbs and grated lemon rind. Cover the pan with a folded cloth and leave aside for 10 minutes.

Make the dressing by crushing the salt, peppercorns and garlic together with a pestle and mortar. Add the mustard, vinegar and olive oil, then shake the whole lot together in a screw-top jar.

Tip the salad ingredients into a bowl, pour the dressing all over and fluff it with a skewer. Serve the salad warm or cold.

Nine herb salad of Hintlesham

(serves 4–6 people)

These are the ingredients used by Robert Carrier at his famous restaurant at Hintlesham Hall in Suffolk. For those who can't get hold of the particular kinds of lettuce, he says other types of green salad vegetable will do. Indeed, I have made this salad successfully using watercress and chopped spinach leaves. And, of course, if you can't get certain herbs, use what's available.

1 salad bowl lettuce
1 Cos lettuce
1 Lamb's lettuce (Mâche)
12 sprigs tarragon
12 sprigs basil
12 sprigs purple basil
12 sprigs pourprier (purslane)
12 sprigs roquette
12 sprigs flat-leafed parsley
Coarsely chopped fennel
Coarsely chopped chives
Coarsely chopped parsley
1 quantity vinaigrette dressing (page 576)

Prepare the various lettuces, and cut the fresh herbs (tarragon, basil, purple basil, pourprier, roquette and flat-leafed parsley) into tiny sprigs about 1 inch (2·5 cm) long. Combine the lettuce leaves with the sprigs of herbs and arrange them in a salad bowl. Pour over the dressing, sprinkle with the coarsely chopped fennel, chives and parsley. Toss well before serving.

Chicken salad with tarragon and grapes

(serves 4–6 people)

This is the perfect main course salad for a warm day, with perhaps some brown rice salad to go with it.

1 cooked chicken, about 3 lb (1·35 kg) or 3¾ lb (1·7 kg) raw weight
5 fl oz home-made mayonnaise (150 ml), (see page 577)
3 fl oz double cream (75 ml)
4 oz green grapes, halved and de-pipped (110 g)
1 heaped teaspoon chopped tarragon—if you can't get hold of fresh tarragon, use ½ heaped teaspoon of dried, soaked in warm water for 5 minutes, then squeezed dry in kitchen paper
3 spring onions
A few sprigs watercress
1 small lettuce
Salt and freshly-milled black pepper

Remove the skin from the chicken and slice the flesh into longish pieces where possible. Remove all the chicken from the bones and place all the meat in a bowl, seasoning with salt and pepper.

In a separate bowl mix the mayonnaise thoroughly with the cream, adding the chopped tarragon and finely chopped spring onions. Now pour the sauce over the chicken, mix it well so that all the chicken pieces get a good coating, then arrange it on a plate of crisp lettuce leaves and garnish with green grapes and a few sprigs of watercress.

Poached trout with herbs

(serves 4 people)

This is very light and a good recipe for slimmers if the parsley butter isn't used for serving.

4 trout, weighing approximately 6 oz each (175 g), cleaned
Salt
6 whole peppercorns
4 bayleaves
1 small onion, peeled and cut into rings
1 lemon

| 1 sprig fresh thyme, or 1 teaspoon dried thyme |
| 3 tablespoons fresh parsley, finely chopped |
| 2 tablespoons fresh snipped chives |
| 4 fl oz dry white wine (110 ml) |
| 3 oz butter (75 g) |

Place the trout in a large frying pan or a thick-based roasting tin. Now sprinkle a little salt over them and throw in the peppercorns. Next add the bayleaves, one in between each trout. Lay onion rings over the top, cut half the lemon into slices and arrange them here and there. Add the thyme and sprinkle a tablespoon of chopped parsley over everything. Finally add the wine and enough cold water just to cover the fish. Bring it to the boil on top of the stove and let it simmer gently, uncovered, for 6 minutes if the trout are fresh or 20 minutes if they are frozen.

Mix the remaining parsley and chives with the butter in a small basin, then divide the mixture into four portions. When the trout are ready, carefully lift them out with a fish slice allowing each one to drain for a few seconds and serve with the parsley butter and the other half of the lemon cut into wedges.

Trout with butter, cream and chives

(serves 2 people)

This recipe is a good one for anyone who has to work and then prepare a meal quickly—the whole thing takes little more than 30 minutes.

| 2 medium trout, 6 or 7 oz each (175 or 200 g), cleaned |
| 1 oz butter (25 g) |
| 3 fl oz double cream (75 ml) |
| 2 tablespoons fresh snipped chives |
| A little extra butter, melted |
| 1 bayleaf |
| Salt and freshly-milled black pepper |

Pre-heat the oven to gas mark 7, 425°F (220°C)

First line a roasting tin with foil and brush it with a little melted butter. Then wash the trout and dry them very thoroughly. Now place them in the roasting tin, brush each one with a little melted butter and season with salt and pepper. Bake them, on a high shelf in the oven, for about 10–15 minutes.

While that's happening empty the cream into a saucepan, add the bayleaf and bring it up to boiling point. Then stir in the chives and the butter, season with salt and pepper, and pour this mixture into a warm jug. Serve it with the fish, some buttered new potatoes and a green salad or some fresh cooked spinach.

Baked mackerel with herb stuffing
(serves 2 people)

Mackerel need to be very fresh so try to buy bright, stiff-looking fish rather than flabby, tired-looking ones.

2 mackerel, gutted and heads removed
2 oz white breadcrumbs (50 g)
1 oz butter (25 g)
3 large spring onions, chopped
The grated rind of half a lemon
2 teaspoons lemon juice
1 tablespoon fresh chopped parsley
1 tablespoon snipped chives
1 teaspoon finely chopped fresh tarragon (or ½ teaspoon dried)
½ teaspoon dried thyme
5 fl oz yoghurt (150 ml)
Salt and freshly-milled black pepper
Oil

Pre-heat the oven to gas mark 5, 375°F (190°C)

Wash and dry the mackerel thoroughly. Start by melting the butter and gently frying the chopped spring onions for about 2 minutes, then combine in the breadcrumbs, lemon rind and juice and half the whole quantity of herbs. Season well with salt and pepper and pack an equal quantity of the mixture into the belly of each fish. Brush the fish with oil and season with salt and freshly-milled pepper. Place them in a foil-lined baking tin and bake in the top half of the oven for 25 minutes.

Stir the remaining herbs into the yoghurt and season with salt and freshly-milled pepper. Pour over the fish and bake for 5 minutes, then serve with some buttery potatoes and a crisp green salad.

Cucumber with soured cream and dill

(serves 2–3 people)

Dill goes well with all cucumber or soured cream recipes. This combines both, and is marvellous with fish.

1 lb cucumber (450 g), cut into ½ inch (1 cm) cubes with the skin left on
1½ oz butter (40 g)
2 spring onions, chopped—including the green tops
1 teaspoon fresh chopped dill or ¼ teaspoon dried dill
2½ fl oz soured cream (65 ml)
1 dessertspoon lemon juice
Salt and freshly-milled black pepper

Heat the butter in a smallish pan and stir in the chopped spring onions. Cook for 2 minutes before tipping in the cucumber. Now give them a good stir to coat with the butter, sprinkle with the dill, then cover and cook over a medium heat for about 8 minutes. Shake the pan now and then to make sure none of the cucumber catches on the base of the pan.

As soon as the pieces are just tender (but still with a bit of 'bite' to them), turn the heat down, stir in the soured cream and a little lemon juice, and season with salt and pepper before serving.

Note: this is also good made with some small, young courgettes.

Pork chops with sage and apples

(serves 4 people)

This is an excellent recipe and a very easy one.

4 lean pork chops
4 tablespoons dried white breadcrumbs
3 level dessertspoons very finely chopped fresh sage or 3 teaspoons dried
1 small egg
1 medium-sized onion, peeled and sliced into rings
1 large cooking apple, peeled and sliced into rings
1 tablespoon butter
2 tablespoons oil
Salt and freshly-milled black pepper
Extra butter and oil

First of all mix the sage and breadcrumbs together and season well with coarsely ground black pepper and salt. Then beat up the egg and dip the pork chops first in the egg, then into the breadcrumb and sage mixture, pressing firmly all round so that the chops get a really good even coating.

Now heat the oil and butter together in a frying pan and, first of all, brown the chops quickly on both sides with the fat fairly hot, then lower the heat and let them gently cook through (it will take around 25–30 minutes depending on the thickness of the chops).

While that's happening, melt a little more butter and oil in another frying pan and fry the apple and onion rings. Drain everything on crumpled greaseproof paper before serving.

Leg of lamb baked with butter and herbs

(serves 4–6 people)

This is an absolute favourite recipe—delicious served with *Redcurrant, orange and mint sauce* in Part One, page 157.

1 leg of lamb weighing about 4 lb (2 kg)
3 oz butter at room temperature (75 g)
1 teaspoon finely chopped rosemary
2 tablespoons fresh chopped mint
2 tablespoons fresh chopped parsley
1 teaspoon fresh chopped thyme
1 clove garlic, crushed
Salt and freshly-milled black pepper

For the gravy:
1 dessertspoon plain flour
3 fl oz dry red or white wine (75 ml)
Approx. ½ pint (275 ml) vegetable stock
Seasoning

Pre-heat the oven to gas mark 5, 375°F (190°C)

Mix the butter, herbs and garlic together, adding a level teaspoon of salt and some freshly-milled black pepper. Stab the joint in several places with a skewer, and rub the herb butter all over the upper side (these stabs with the skewer will allow the butter to run into the joint during the cooking).

Now wrap the joint loosely in foil, sealing well. Place it in a meat roasting tin and cook it for 2 hours, then open out the foil and cook it for a further 30 minutes to brown nicely. With these cooking times the lamb will be slightly pink. If you like it well done give it a little extra time in the foil before opening it out. To serve, remove the joint to a warm serving dish and leave it in a warm place while you make the gravy.

Empty the juices from the foil into the roasting tin, then tilt it slightly. You will see the meat juices and the fat separating, so spoon off most of the fat into a bowl and leave the juices in the tin. Now place the tin over a medium heat, and when the juices start to bubble, sprinkle in the flour and work it to a smooth paste using a wooden spoon, then cook it for a minute or so to brown. Now pour in the wine and stock by degrees, stirring continuously and adding just enough stock to make a thin gravy. Taste to check the seasoning, pour into a jug and serve with the lamb.

Cream cheese with herbs

(serves 4 people)

6 oz cream cheese (175 g)
2 spring onions, very finely chopped
2 tablespoons fresh chopped parsley
1 tablespoon fresh snipped chives
1 level teaspoon chopped tarragon
1 level teaspoon chopped thyme
1 clove garlic, crushed
Freshly-milled black pepper and salt (if it needs it)

Combine all the above ingredients together in a basin, then form the cheese into a round cake-shape, and serve it for lunch with lots of fresh crusty bread and a crisp salad.

Summer vegetables

Including recipes for:
Broad bean purée
Baby broad beans in parsley sauce
Broccoli fritters
Courgettes and tomatoes au gratin
Braised fennel
Baked marrow with tomatoes and coriander
Mushrooms in hot garlic butter
Braised peas with lettuce and spring onions
New Jersey potatoes with fresh herb butter
Spinach and cheese sauce
Baked spinach with brown rice and cheese
Eggs Florentine
Turkish stuffed tomatoes
Glazed baby turnips

For me one of the simple pleasures of the summer and the early autumn is to wander among the vegetable stalls in a market and wonder at the magnificent array of summer crops. I love to see carrots in bunches with their dark feathery tops, tender young peas in fresh squeaky pods, tight green cabbages and creamy white baby turnips. But on a practical level too, the sheer range of choice for the cook makes the preparation of family meals so much more pleasurable.

However, on the question of choice, the buyer of vegetables is at something of a disadvantage compared with those who are able to grow them at home or on an allotment. Quite apart from the strange regulations imposed by the Common Market, the market gardener will tend to choose varieties that can be grown for their heavy cropping—and this is by no means the same as growing vegetables for their flavour. The home-grower need have no such limitations. I would dearly love some enterprising firm to offer us, on a commercial basis, a choice of vegetables based on quality rather than quantity; but having said that, we are still very lucky in this country. We may have to put up with imported vegetables in the winter, but in the summer buying British really is best.

In the notes which follow I have recommended some varieties of different vegetables. These suggestions are largely for the benefit of the home-grower. Unfortunately, they may not all be readily available in the market at present. Once again this is something that only we, the consumers, can do anything about, by insisting that we want the vegetables that *taste* best.

Globe artichokes

It would be hard to find a prettier vegetable than this: its aesthetic presence animates any table display. Although they were once very popular in Britain, the biggest crop now comes from Brittany in the late spring. It may be, with the waning of their popularity, that people do not know how to prepare and eat them. So first let me explain that globe artichokes are—as indeed they look—large members of the thistle family, and have three distinct parts. There are the leaves (the bottom parts of which are edible), the choke (which is inedible) and the heart which is very edible.

How to prepare and cook artichokes First remove about four of the toughest outer leaves, then place the artichoke at the edge of a table so that the stalk overlaps the edge. Grasp the stalk and snap away the stem, removing also some of the tough fibres running up into the base. Now remove the inedible choke: carefully spread the leaves apart until you come to the central cone of thinner, lightly-coloured leaves. Then pull this cone out in one piece and underneath it you'll find the hairy 'choke'—scrape this all out of the heart with a teaspoon, and add a little lemon juice to stop the inside discolouring. Now rinse out the artichokes and leave them upside down in some cold water to which some more lemon juice has been added (about 1 tablespoon to 2 pints (1·25 l) of water), until you are ready to cook them.

Don't boil artichokes in iron or aluminium pans, as this can discolour them. Have your chosen pan ready filled with salted boiling water with a tablespoon of lemon juice (or white wine vinegar) added. Gently boil the artichokes, uncovered, for about 30–40 minutes or until one of the outer leaves pulls away easily and the bases feel tender when tested with a skewer. Then drain the artichokes upside down in a colander, shaking them to get rid of the excess water.

How to eat artichokes This does have its comic side, with ever-mounting piles of discarded leaves scarred with rabbit-toothed marks! Artichokes can be served cold or, perhaps better, just tepid. Tear off one leaf at a time, dip it into the sauce (see below), and eat the tender rounded part at the base. When you arrive at the heart, cut it into sections with a knife and fork and eat with the rest of the sauce. Don't forget to have plenty of napkins, some finger bowls, and a large plate for the discarded leaves.

Sauces for artichokes To serve warm, I would recommend *Quick Hollandaise* (Part One, page 39) or *Hot lemon butter*, which is simply the juice and grated rind of a lemon plus 6 oz (175 g) butter, melted together until bubbling and poured immediately into the cavity of each artichoke. For serving cold, I suggest either *Vinaigrette* (page 576) or some *Home-made mayonnaise* with garlic (page 577).

Asparagus

Asparagus (or 'grass' as it's known in the trade) is a very regal vegetable. While the carefully graded bunches of matching spears might sometimes seem an expensive luxury, the loose ungraded asparagus can be reasonable at the height of the (short) season. I'm no gardener, but some time ago I planted some 2-year-old crowns and now asparagus obligingly appears in profusion during May and June all by itself. Those few stalks that are really too thin

to be picked up with the fingers can be used in a quiche or with
Eggs en cocotte with soured cream and asparagus (see page 553).

To cook asparagus Steaming is the only way to cook asparagus—its
flavour is so delicate I'm absolutely against ever putting it into
water. You can buy specially shaped asparagus steamers, but I
find it hard to justify the expense. An ordinary steamer (as used for
steamed puddings) will do very well. Trim the stalks down to a
reasonable length, 8–9 inches (20–23 cm), fit them inside the
steamer and sprinkle them with salt. Place the steamer over a
saucepan of boiling water and let the asparagus cook for 8–12
minutes, depending on the thickness of the stalks. Meanwhile heat
up some butter in a pan to the frothy stage, and when the
asparagus is ready serve it on hot plates with the butter poured
over (and some crusty bread to mop up the juices afterwards).
Alternatively you can serve it with *Hollandaise sauce* (see Part One,
page 151), which will keep warm in a bowl over a pan of barely
simmering water. Don't forget the napkins and finger-bowls.
Note: 2 lb (900 g) of asparagus is a very ample serving for 4 people.

Beans
Broad Beans These are the first beans of spring and are at their best,
I think, when they're young and tender. So many people claim not
to like them because they have only tasted the old (probably
over-boiled) toughies. On one memorable occasion I ate them in a
Chinese restaurant filleted, with the skins peeled off. Now I would
never have the patience to do that, but for those who grow their
own I would recommend that they harvest some of the immature
pods (not more than finger-thick) and try cooking them
whole—see the recipe on page 639. Shelled broad beans need very
light cooking, just 6–8 minutes, and are delicious served tossed in
Herb butter (see Part One page 163) or else in a salad with bacon
(see page 593).

   For a lovely *Broad bean purée* (for 2–3 people): shell 2 lb (900 g)
beans, and cook them for 6–8 minutes in salted water. Drain them
well, then place them in the goblet of a liquidiser together with
1 oz (25 g) butter, 2½ fl oz (65 ml) single cream, some pepper and
nutmeg and whizz them to a purée. Taste to check the seasoning,
and serve with a few snipped chives sprinkled over. These go very
well with pork sausages.

Dwarf beans These are sometimes called *haricots verts* (tiny flat baby
beans) or Bobby beans (which are actually rounder and larger).

Top and tail them with scissors, and cook in boiling salted water for about 4–6 minutes if they're really tiny, 8–12 minutes if larger. I like to drain them, put them back in the pan and toss with olive oil, a little crushed garlic and pepper and salt before serving.

Runner beans Is there anyone who doesn't love these? They are, in my opinion, superior in flavour to any of the other beans, and for that reason I would supplement them with nothing more than salt and pepper, and perhaps a little butter. To prepare them, use a sharp paring knife to top and tail them, and pare away the stringy edge along the seams of each bean. Slice them thinly, diagonally (an operation which, I've come to the conclusion, is really done best with a bean slicer—the kind with a handle). Boil them in salted water for 5 minutes or so, depending on their age.

Baby broad beans in parsley sauce

(serves 4 people)

This recipe is for gardeners who can pick their broad beans very young—no more than finger thick—and cook them, chopped, in their pods.

1 lb young broad beans (450 g)
2 oz butter (50 g)
1½ oz flour (40 g)
½ pint milk (275 ml)
4 tablespoons fresh chopped parsley
An extra ½ oz butter (10 g)
1 teaspoon lemon juice
Salt and freshly-milled black pepper

First wash, top and tail the beans then cut them into ½ inch (1 cm) lengths. Place them in a saucepan, pour in enough boiling water to just cover, and add some salt. Cover and when they come to the boil, simmer them for about 10 minutes.

Meanwhile start to make the sauce by melting the butter in a small saucepan, add the flour and beat until smooth. Then gradually add the milk, beating until smooth after each addition. Allow the mixture to cook for a few minutes over a gentle heat. Now when the beans are cooked, strain the cooking liquid into a jug. Drain the beans well and place them in a warm serving dish.

Then quickly beat 5 fl oz (150 ml) of the cooking liquid into the sauce—again gradually. Season to taste with salt, pepper and lemon juice, then throw in the parsley and stir in the extra ½ oz (10 g) of butter. Serve the beans with the sauce poured over.

Broccoli

Sprouting broccoli—purple or white—and calabrese, which is the wider curly-headed variety, can be used in precisely the same way as cauliflower (see for instance, *Sautéed cauliflower with coriander* Part One, page 191). The leafy sprouting heads can be either boiled or steamed briefly then finished off by tossing in butter with salt and pepper. For a light, wafer-crispness, try deep-frying the small heads—as in the following recipe.

Broccoli fritters

(serves 2–3 people)

You could, in fact, also use thinly sliced courgettes in this recipe for crisp fritters.

---

8 oz small broccoli sprigs (225 g)—if you buy 1 lb (450 g) you should be able to pick off the correct weight of sprigs

2 egg whites

2 level tablespoons plain flour

Oil for frying—ideally olive oil, otherwise groundnut oil

To serve:

1 teaspoon crushed sea salt and coarsely ground black pepper

Fill a deep fryer or else a largish saucepan to one-third of its capacity with oil, and start to heat it up to 360°F (185°C)—or until a cube of bread turns golden in 60 seconds. Meanwhile crumple some greaseproof paper and lay it in a serving dish, and keep this warm. Now whisk the egg whites to the stiff peak stage, then coat the broccoli sprigs, first in the flour, then in the beaten egg white. Deep-fry them—in two batches—shaking the pan gently and using a knife to stir the sprigs around and separate them. 2–3 minutes for each batch should be enough, so the whole operation is fairly quick. Then drain them on the crumpled greaseproof paper, sprinkle with crushed sea salt and coarse pepper and serve immediately or they'll lose their crispness.

Corn-on-the-cob

This is something I've never grown myself, but a more green-fingered neighbour always lets me have some of his surplus cobs, and once a year we have a feast (on our own, getting faces and fingers smothered in butter and sharing a damp tea-towel). On the streets of Istanbul, I recall, every corner seemed to have corn-on-the-cobs being grilled over open charcoal fires, and groups of people standing round munching their way through them!

At home we boil the cobs. First remove the husks and fibrous bits, then wash the cobs and plunge them into boiling water (10 minutes is usually sufficient). Test the kernels for tenderness with a skewer, then drain well and have some hot melted butter and hot plates handy. Pour some butter over each cob, and season well with salt and coarsely-ground black pepper. They are easiest to eat if you stick small skewers or forks into each end, and use these to hold them. And if you want to be more refined than us, have some finger-bowls and linen napkins on the table.

Spring carrots
The first baby carrots of the spring are an unrivalled treat. We grow a variety called Early Nantes, which have the sweetest flavour and fragrance. When you're buying 'bunch' carrots your supplier may offer to cut off the tops, but I think these are better left on until you're ready to cook them (somehow this seems to keep them fresher). Don't scrape new carrots—just rinse each one under a cold tap—and when you're cooking them, pour boiling water over (but not too much), add some salt, then watch them like a hawk for 10–20 minutes, depending on their thickness. Test them with a skewer—they should be tender but under no circumstances soggy.

Spring carrots with tarragon butter
Use 1 teaspoonful of chopped tarragon leaves to 3 oz (75 g) butter, add some salt and freshly-milled pepper, mix together thoroughly, then melt this over 1 lb (450 g) carrots just before serving.

Carrots with spring onions and cream
Finely chop 3 spring onions and add them to 2 tablespoons of cream (single or double) together with some seasoning. Toss the hot, drained carrots in this mixture just before serving.

Courgettes
Courgettes (or zucchini) are the easiest vegetables in the world to grow—and perhaps the hardest to stop growing! If you don't inspect them every day during their season you will end up with mature marrows, rather than baby ones (which is what courgettes

really are). Like their elders, they do contain a fair amount of water and sometimes this can be bitter. So if you have the time, prepare them by slicing them thinly into rounds (always leaving the skin on), then layer them in a colander sprinkling each layer with salt, and place a suitably-sized plate on top. Weight this down with a heavy object (like scale weights), and after 30 minutes quite a bit of water will have been drawn out. Dry them really thoroughly in a clean cloth, and then they're ready to cook. I prefer not to put any water near them—just fry them in a mixture of butter and olive oil for about 7 minutes (rather like sautéed potatoes), so that the edges turn crisp and golden.

Courgette fritters
For these, cut the courgettes into 2 inch (5 cm) lengths (skins on), then cut each length in half horizontally, and cut each half into chip-like lengths. Salt and drain these as above, dry well, then cook in exactly the same way as *Broccoli fritters* (see page 640).

Courgettes and tomatoes au gratin
(serves 2–4 people)

This is a very quick and easy supper dish for 2 people, especially good if you grow your own tomatoes and courgettes and have a glut to use up. You could also serve it as a 'starter' for 4 people.

4 medium courgettes, sliced but *not* peeled
2 tablespoons olive oil
4 large tomatoes, skinned and sliced
1 large clove garlic, crushed
1 rounded teaspoon dried oregano
4 level tablespoons Parmesan cheese, grated
4 oz Cheddar cheese, grated (110 g)
Salt and freshly-milled black pepper

Pre-heat the oven to gas mark 5, 375°F (190°C)

If you have the time salt, drain and dry the sliced courgettes as described above. Heat the oil in a frying pan large enough to hold the courgettes in one layer (otherwise do them in two batches), add the crushed garlic and sauté the courgette slices to a nice golden colour on each side. Next arrange layers of courgettes and the skinned and sliced tomatoes in a heatproof gratin dish, sprinkling each layer with grated Parmesan, oregano and salt and freshly-milled pepper. Finish with a layer of the tomatoes, sprinkle the Cheddar cheese all over, and bake on a high shelf in the oven for 30 minutes. Serve this with lots of crusty wholemeal bread and butter and a crisp lettuce salad.

Fennel
Fennel has been dealt with primarily in the chapter on Salads (see page 582), but it is also extremely good served as a vegetable. When cooked the aniseed flavour is definitely less pronounced.

Braised fennel
(serves 4 people)

This is a vegetable that's served both raw in salad and cooked as a vegetable in Italy. In the 18th century it was used quite a lot in English cooking, so let's hope it will become popular here again.

4 bulbs fennel, uniform size if possible
2 slices streaky bacon, rind removed
1 oz butter (25 g)
1 carrot, sliced
Half an onion, sliced
5 fl oz cooking water (150 ml)
Chopped parsley
Salt and freshly-milled black pepper

First trim the green shoots from the tops of the fennel bulbs and shave off the bases. Then peel off any outer layers if they seem brownish, and halve the bulbs across their widest part. Put them into a large saucepan of boiling water, bring to the boil again and blanch for 3 or 4 minutes. Then drain them—reserving 5 fl oz (150 ml) of the water.

Now fry the bacon in the butter in a large saucepan or casserole, stir in the sliced vegetables and cook for a few minutes before pouring in the reserved water and adding some salt and freshly-milled black pepper. Arrange the fennel in the base of the pan, bring to simmering point, cover and cook gently for about 45 minutes, turning the fennel occasionally.

When cooked, transfer to a serving dish along with the vegetables, bacon and some of the juices. Sprinkle with parsley and serve.

Mange tout

These are a real summer delicacy—tiny under-developed peas
that are cooked and served in their pods. In cooking them there
are two important points to bear in mind: on no account should
they be over-cooked—the end results should be really crunchy,
and they should not be allowed even a sniff of water. Top and tail
the pods. Melt 2 oz (50 g) of butter in a wide, shallow saucepan (or
a frying pan), stir in 1 lb (450 g) of mange tout gently to get each
one coated in the butter, add some salt, and then just toss them
around over a medium heat. You'll find they cook very quickly,
just 1–2 minutes.

Marrow

If you grow courgettes then you're bound to find that some have
remained hidden from view under the large flat leaves—and
before you know it you have a young marrow on your hands. If so,
then pick it immediately because the older monsters aren't much
good for anything. If you are buying a marrow the same rule
applies: small is beautiful, not more than 1½–2 lb (700–900 g). The
way to tell a young marrow—apart from its size—is to look for a
shiny skin, and when you press along one of the ridges with your
thumb, it should leave an impression.

Young marrow should be cut up into large 1½ inch (4 cm) cubes
(with the skin left on) and cooked, sprinkled with salt, in a steamer
over simmering water until tender. Serve it with a *Herb butter* (see
Part One, page 163) or, better still, as in the following recipe.

Baked marrow with tomatoes and coriander

(serves 4 people)

If, like me, you've sometimes suffered
from rather too many home-grown
marrows—do try this way of cooking
them—which also takes care of any
tomatoes that are too ripe for a salad.

1½ lb young marrow (700 g)
8 oz red ripe tomatoes (about 4 medium-sized ones), skinned and chopped (225 g)
Half a medium-sized onion, chopped
1 clove garlic, crushed
½ teaspoon whole coriander seeds, crushed in a pestle and mortar or with the back of a tablespoon

| 1 dessertspoon fresh chopped basil (or 1 level teaspoon dried) |
| Oil |
| Salt and freshly-milled black pepper |

Pre-heat the oven to gas mark 3, 325°F (170°C)

Melt a tablespoon of oil in a flameproof casserole, add the onion and garlic, and soften them over a gentle heat for 5 minutes. Stir in the chopped tomatoes and cook for a further 5 minutes.

If the marrow is young and fresh it won't need peeling, just cut it into approximately 1½ inch (4 cm) chunks. Add them to the tomatoes and onions along with the crushed coriander seeds. Then add the basil if it's dried (if you're using fresh basil, add it at the end), and season with salt and pepper. Stir everything around well, put a lid on, and place the casserole in the oven to cook for 1 hour or until the marrow is tender. About 10 minutes before the end of the cooking time, put the casserole back on the top of the stove and simmer without a lid to reduce some of the liquid.

Note: this is equally good served cold—or reheated the next day.

Mushrooms

The best mushrooms I've ever tasted were those gathered on early-morning walks through the mountains in Wales, as a small child. My grandfather seemed able to spot a field mushroom from dozens of yards away, and I would run and pick them—some small, round and delicate with pink gills, others large and flat and velvet-brown. Back at home they would sizzle in bacon fat for breakfast, with plenty of bread to mop up the last traces of juice.

Field mushrooms are still a delicious, if rare, treat. Cultivated mushrooms are not quite the same, but at least they are plentiful, always available and not too expensive. I rarely use the 'button' variety, which I find rather tasteless. I much prefer the fully-opened caps with pink or brown gills. One of the nicest mushroom-flavoured recipes is *Marinaded mushrooms* (see page 521), which makes a very good first course. For a really concentrated mushroom flavour—for sauces, stuffing or quiches—make what the French call *Duxelles* (see, for instance, the *Boeuf en croûte* in Part One, page 92 and the *Cheese tartlets with mushroom pâté* in Part Two, page 479).

Duxelles

Heat 1 oz (25 g) butter in a saucepan, stir in 1 medium-sized onion very finely chopped, and cook for 5 minutes. Chop 8 oz (225 g) mushrooms very finely, add these to the pan, and cook gently for 30 minutes (uncovered) so that all the liquid evaporates and the mixture becomes a thick paste. Season with salt, pepper and a grating of nutmeg.

Mushrooms in hot garlic butter

(serves 4 people)

This recipe is for people who, like me, love the sizzling garlic butter that goes with snails but cannot eat the snails.

1 lb mushrooms (450 g)
6 oz butter, at room temperature (175 g)
2 large cloves garlic, crushed
1 tablespoon lemon juice
1–2 tablespoons fresh chopped parsley
Salt and freshly-milled black pepper

Pre-heat the oven to gas mark 7, 425°F (220°C)

Begin by preparing the mushrooms simply by wiping them with kitchen paper, then pull off the stalks—but don't discard them. Now, in a small basin, combine the crushed garlic with the butter, and stir in the parsley and lemon juice. Season the mixture with salt and freshly-milled black pepper.

Next arrange the mushroom caps, skin side down, in a gratin dish or roasting tin, with the stalks arranged among them. Place a little of the garlic butter mixture into each cap, and spread whatever remains over the stalks as well.

Now place the dish on the top shelf of the pre-heated oven, and let them cook for 10–15 minutes or until the butter is sizzling away and the mushrooms look slightly toasted. Serve straight from the oven with lashings of crusty bread to mop up the garlicky juices.

Onions (and shallots)

On the subject of preparing onions, I would like to say that in my 17 years of cooking I have been regaled with countless theories on how not to cry. None of them have worked! I do now own a food-processor, which chops onions finely, so perhaps I don't weep as much as I used to. The mildest onions are the large Spanish type, and these are good for slicing and eating raw in salads. It is the medium-sized home-grown variety that are the real tear-jerkers.

Shallots—I grow the purple shallots—keep very well through the winter if stored correctly. Usually they are mild flavoured, and especially good for cooking whole in a number of recipes. I make a habit of pickling some shallots for Christmas—and the recipe for that is on page 667.

Crisp-fried onion rings

First you need to heat some oil in a deep-fryer to 350°F (180°C). Slice 2 onions into thinnish rings and separate out the rings. Beat up 1 large egg white to the stiff peak stage, then dip the rings first into seasoned plain flour, then into the egg white. Deep-fry them a few at a time until crisp and golden (1–2 minutes). Drain on some crumpled greaseproof paper, and serve as soon as possible. These are lovely served with steak or liver.

Peas

I hear some people now saying they actually prefer frozen peas to fresh peas, because those bought in the pods from supermarkets are so often hard and old. It's quite true that growers—and I live among many of them—have found the demand from freezing companies more lucrative, and growing peas to sell fresh has become uneconomical. But nothing will convince me that the uniform frozen peas can ever compare with those freshly-picked, mouthwateringly tender and sweet. The answer, as always, is for us to keep asking for fresh peas, and then they will come back.

The best way to cook them is briefly. Pour boiling water into the pan to reach halfway up the peas, add some salt, cook and in just a couple of minutes, your peas will be ready. I don't find it necessary to add mint or butter, or anything to add to their flavour. If the peas you have grown, or bought, happen to be getting on a bit, the following recipe is good for braising them into tenderness.

Braised peas with lettuce and spring onions

(serves 4 people)

This is a very good recipe for using fresh shelled peas that are not so young.

2 lb peas (900 g), freshly shelled (weight before shelling)
6 lettuce leaves
8 spring onions

| 2 oz butter (50 g) |
| 4 tablespoons water |
| A pinch of sugar |
| 1 level teaspoon salt |

Trim the onions—you only need the bulbous white part—and break the lettuce leaves into wide strips. Then melt the butter in a thick-based saucepan, add the onions, lettuce and peas. Stir well, then add the water, sugar and salt. Bring to simmering point, then cover the saucepan and let it cook over a very, very gentle heat for about 20–25 minutes (keeping an eye on the pan, and shaking it now and then to prevent the vegetables sticking). Add just a little more water if you think it needs it.

New Potatoes

Around April we begin to get the first imported new potatoes, by which time the old ones are looking decidedly wrinkled and sprouty. However these very early imported potatoes are often disappointing in flavour, and it's only when our home-grown varieties start to make an appearance that their true delicacy can be appreciated—and that goes especially for the Jersey Royals.

Freshness is the key to buying new potatoes. Pick one up before you buy and rub your thumb along it—if the skin slips away with your thumb, you can be sure the potatoes are really fresh.

To prepare them, all you actually need to do is to rinse them clean under a cold tap. Don't scrape or peel them, because the skins are full of flavour and nutrients.

New potatoes also deserve careful cooking: what I do is place the largest ones on the base of the pan, with the smaller ones on top. Add some salt, and pour in enough boiling water to come not more than three-quarters of the way up (so that, in effect, the smallest potatoes are cooked in the steam and will be ready at about the same time as the larger ones). Use a tight-fitting lid, and test with a skewer to see if they are cooked after about 20 minutes.

New Jersey potatoes with fresh herb butter

(serves 4 people)

No new potatoes can ever taste as good as Jersey Royals in my opinion—they're so good I could eat them just by themselves. Because they're rather expensive they need careful cooking, and this is a delicious way to serve them.

2 lb Jersey potatoes (900 g)
1 sprig fresh mint
3 oz butter (75 g)
1 tablespoon fresh chopped parsley
2 tablespoons fresh chopped mint
1 tablespoon fresh snipped chives
Salt (ideally rock salt) and freshly-milled black pepper

Wash, but don't scrape, the potatoes as there are a lot of nutrients as well as flavour in the skins. Place the larger ones over the base of the saucepan and pop the smaller ones on top. Pour in enough boiling water to not quite cover, add some salt and a sprig of mint. Cover with a tight-fitting lid, and simmer gently for about 20–25 minutes. Test them with a skewer, and remember they must be tender but still firm—over-cooking really does spoil them. Meanwhile mix the butter and herbs thoroughly together with some pepper. Then drain the cooked potatoes, add the herb butter, put the lid back on and swirl the pan around to get each one thoroughly coated. Remove the lid and just savour the delicious aroma for a couple of seconds before you dish them out!

Spinach

A very versatile vegetable, spinach—and there's something very wholesome about it when the leaves are young, fresh and squeaky. Fresh spinach can be rather dusty or muddy, so the best way to deal with this is to fill the sink with cold water, pick out any damaged or brown leaves and remove any tough stalks, then plunge the rest in the water and swirl them around. Do this in 2–3 changes of water, then let it all drain in a colander, shaking it well over the sink. Young spinach leaves can be wiped and used raw in a delicious salad (see page 585). When cooked, spinach loses roughly half its weight—so 1 lb (450 g) of spinach is enough for 2 people.

Spinach has plenty of moisture in it, so it needs no water at all for cooking. For 1 lb (450 g) of spinach leaves, melt 1 oz (25 g) butter in a thick-based saucepan, then keeping the heat at medium, pack the spinach leaves in. Add some salt, put on a tight-fitting lid, and let it cook for about 30 seconds. Then take the lid off and you'll find the spinach has collapsed down into the butter. Give it a stir so that the top leaves get pushed down to the base of the pan, replace the lid and give it another 30 seconds or so, shaking the pan a couple of times—I find the whole operation takes less than 2 minutes. Next drain the spinach in a colander, pressing it well with a saucer to get rid of any excess water. You can now return it to the pan, and season with freshly-milled pepper and—best of all—nutmeg. Add a bit more butter or, if you like, a tablespoon of fresh cream.

Spinach and cheese sauce

This is a delicious, colourful sauce to pour over halved hard-boiled eggs on a bed of brown rice, or to accompany any grilled or fried fish. Cook 8 oz (225 g) fresh spinach leaves as above, then place them in a liquidiser with a cheese sauce made with 2 oz (50 g) butter, 1 oz (25 g) plain flour, ½ pint (275 ml) milk, 3 oz (75 g) grated cheese, and 2 tablespoons double cream. Liquidise until you have a pale-green, speckled sauce. Season with salt, pepper and freshly grated nutmeg, and re-heat before serving.

Baked spinach with brown rice and cheese

(serves 2–3 people)

For this meatless supper dish you can use either fresh or frozen spinach.

1 lb fresh spinach leaves, washed and chopped, (450 g) or ½ lb frozen spinach, thawed (225 g)
Brown rice measured to the 8 fl oz level in a measuring jug
16 fl oz hot water
1 onion, finely chopped
1 tablespoon oil
1 teaspoon butter
4 oz grated Cheddar cheese (110 g)
2 large eggs, beaten
2 tablespoons chopped parsley
2 tablespoons wholewheat breadcrumbs
1 tablespoon melted butter
Couple of pinches cayenne
Nutmeg
Salt and freshly-milled black pepper

Pre-heat the oven to gas mark 4, 350°F (180°C)

Melt the butter and oil in a saucepan and soften the onion in it, then stir in the rice to get it nicely coated with oil. Add the hot water, stir once, and simmer gently with a lid on for 40 minutes or until the liquid has been absorbed and the grains are tender.

As soon as the rice is cooked, cool it in a bowl, then combine it with the grated cheese, and stir in the eggs and parsley followed by the chopped spinach. Season well and add a good grating of nutmeg. Now place the mixture into a large oiled pie dish, mix the breadcrumbs with the melted butter and cayenne and sprinkle that over the top. Bake in the oven for about 35 minutes.

Eggs Florentine

(serves 2 people)

This is a very quick supper or lunch dish for 2 people. Some recipes call for hard-boiled eggs but I think they taste far nicer baked in with the spinach.

1 lb fresh spinach, cooked (450 g) or 8 oz frozen spinach, thawed (225 g)— either should be well drained
4 large fresh eggs
1 oz plain flour (25 g)
1½ oz butter (40 g)
½ pint milk (275 ml)
2 tablespoons double cream
3 oz grated Lancashire cheese (75 g)
1 oz grated Parmesan cheese (25 g)
Salt and freshly-milled black pepper
Nutmeg
A little extra butter

Pre-heat the oven to gas mark 5, 375°F (190°C)

First butter a large shallow baking dish generously, arrange the cooked spinach over the base, season with pepper, a little salt and freshly grated nutmeg. Then sprinkle 1 tablespoon of cream over and pop the dish in the lower part of the oven to heat through.

Now place the butter, milk and flour in a saucepan and whisk over heat to make a smooth white sauce. Then stir in the grated Lancashire cheese and cook the sauce for 3 minutes over a very gentle heat—stirring now and then.

Now take the baking dish out of the oven, make four depressions in the spinach and gently break the eggs into each one (I like to sprinkle just a little salt and pepper onto the yolks). Stir the remaining tablespoon of cream into the cheese sauce and pour it over the eggs to cover everything completely. Sprinkle with Parmesan, add a few flecks of butter here and there and bake on a high shelf in the oven for 15–20 minutes.

Tomatoes

Here I would like to make a personal plea to tomato-growers. Please could we have some choice of variety? And—just as potatoes now have to be labelled according to variety—could not tomatoes be identified also? The growers have always claimed that the average consumer, whoever that is, wants a uniform size (i.e. eight toms to the pound); and since boring old 'Moneymaker' and similar varieties obligingly conform to this, that's what we get. In fact I can hardly believe this premise to be true—after all what is the difference between two large tomatoes cut into quarters and four small ones halved?

There's another problem too. Most commercial tomatoes are harvested before they have fully ripened, and therefore tend to become pithy and woolly inside. It's no wonder that people who travel on the continent take on a wistful look when speaking about French or Italian tomatoes. (Mind you, I would point out that just because a tomato is large and misshapen, it is not automatically better, it depends on the variety and the soil in which it is grown.)

At home we have grown a small outdoor bush variety called Little Pixie, which produces very sweet tomatoes (and you don't have to pinch out the leaves). I have even seen these grown in window boxes and grow bags. For more experienced home tomato-growers, I would recommend a variety called Ware Cross (which my grandfather used to grow)—lovely deep red fruits with sweet green centres. For the shop-bought varieties you need a well-flavoured salad dressing (see *Tomato salad*, page 584) or when cooking them a gutsy, well-seasoned recipe. *Note:* if you have a lot of green tomatoes at the end of the season, see *Spiced green tomato sauce* (Part One, page 157) and *Green tomato chutney* (page 660).

Turkish *stuffed tomatoes* (serves 4–8 people)	These are good for a light lunch-time dish with salad for 4 people, or this quantity will also serve 8 people as a 'starter'.

Right: Turkish stuffed tomatoes, this page; Country pâté, page 527.

8 really large ripe tomatoes
Italian rice, measured to 5 fl oz level in a measuring jug
1 small onion, finely chopped
1 clove garlic, crushed
1 tablespoon pine nuts (available at Greek or healthfood shops)
1 tablespoon currants
1 teaspoon fresh thyme
1 teaspoon ground cinnamon
10 fl oz hot stock or water (275 ml)
Olive oil
Some sugar
Salt and freshly-milled black pepper

Pre-heat the oven to gas mark 4, 350°F (180°C)

Begin by cooking the rice: fry the onion in a tablespoon of olive oil in a saucepan until softened, then add the crushed garlic and pour in the rice. Add the cinnamon, pine nuts and the currants and give everything a good stir to get it well coated. Then season with some salt and pepper and pour in the hot stock. Stir just once, cover with a lid and let it simmer gently for 15–20 minutes or until all the liquid has been absorbed and the grains of rice are tender. Then remove the rice from the heat, add the thyme and fluff it with a skewer.

Prepare the tomatoes by slicing off a little of the round end and scooping out all the core and seeds—trying to leave as much of the actual flesh as possible. Put a pinch of sugar into each hollowed-out tomato, then pack each one with the rice mixture and replace the lids. Place the tomatoes in a meat roasting tin with a little water in the bottom, drizzle a few drops of olive oil over each one and bake for 25–30 minutes. They are lovely eaten hot or cold. There is a photograph of them on page 653.

Baby Turnips

These are small turnips—about the size of golf balls—creamy white with leafy green tops, usually sold in bunches. When older and larger, they add lots of flavour to *Cornish pasty pie* (see Part One, page 87).

Left: Pork chops with sage and apples, page 632.

Buttered turnips

Peel 1 lb (450 g) turnips and dice them into fairly small cubes. Now blanch them in boiling water for 3 minutes, drain well, then finish off by tossing them in 3 oz (75 g) melted butter in a large frying pan—keeping the heat fairly gentle so they don't brown (5 minutes should be long enough). Serve them sprinkled with snipped chives or chopped parsley.

Glazed baby turnips
(serves 4 people)

2 lb young turnips (900 g)
Some light stock
1 teaspoon Dijon mustard
2 tablespoons dry white wine or dry cider
1 level teaspoon sugar
Chopped parsley
Salt and freshly-milled black pepper

First of all prepare the turnips by peeling them carefully, then put them into a saucepan of boiling salted water and boil for 3 minutes. Next drain in a colander and then return them to the saucepan. Now add just enough stock to cover the turnips, bring this to the boil and simmer (uncovered) for about 10 minutes, or until the turnips are tender. Use a draining spoon to remove the turnips, place them in a warmed serving dish and keep hot while you make the glaze.

Next blend the mustard with a little of the white wine and add to the stock in the saucepan with the remainder of the wine and the sugar. Re-heat, taste and season with salt and freshly-milled pepper. Simmer rapidly (without a lid) until the liquid has reduced to a syrupy consistency, then pour this syrup over the turnips, sprinkle with plenty of chopped parsley and serve.

Preserving

Including recipes for:

Green tomato chutney
Spiced plum chutney
Old Doverhouse chutney
Sweet piccalilli
Victoria plum or damson ketchup
Cranberry and orange relish
Quick pickled onions
Pickled red cabbage
Strawberry jam
Loganberry jam
Damson jam
Plum jam
Blackcurrant jam
Seville orange marmalade
Quick bramble jelly
Redcurrant jelly
Home-made Christmas mincemeat
Uncle Billy's toffee

The British have always been particularly good at preserving and pickling (just as we have excelled at smoking and curing). We have always been fortunate in this country to be able to grow a wide range of fruits and vegetables, beyond our immediate needs, and so have mastered the arts of storing up produce for the dreary winter months. We even exported our enthusiasm abroad—to India, for example—and came back with all manner of chutneys. You can still see the legacy of this passion at our local flower show—and doubtless at shows all over the country—where multi-coloured mountains of neatly-labelled jars stand awaiting inspection and judgement.

Perhaps the necessity to preserve food is no longer so pressing, but the pleasure remains. There's no doubt that strawberry jam spread on a crumpet or fresh-baked scone does bring the memory of a sunny June into the greyness of January, and some dark, spicy plum chutney served with cold ham can remind us that the fruitfulness of autumn can be savoured throughout the year. Most shop-bought jams, with their decided lack of fruit and surfeit of sweetness, or blandly uniform pickles, somehow fail to evoke any such pleasurable dream. All this combined with soaring prices in the shops provides good reasons for making these items at home. And anyone who cares about real food and real flavour won't grudge the time spent on preserving, when a spoonful of faintly sharp and fruity damson jam can put bread-and-jam into the luxury class, or some spicy home-made plum sauce can utterly transform a modest meal of bangers and mash.

General Equipment

Contrary to what you might think, preserving at home does not call for a whole battery of special equipment. Below is a list of the general items which will come in very useful.

Preserving pans A heavy-gauge aluminium preserving pan is a good investment—it's large, sturdy, and will last a lifetime. Its biggest asset is its size, since it will hold more than most family-sized saucepans. It is also very wide and open at the top which means (in the case of chutney-making) the vinegar can reduce more effectively. Perhaps I ought to emphasise 'open' here, because I recall one distressed reader phoning the paper I worked for, saying she had been simmering her chutney for a whole day and it still hadn't reduced. On phoning her back I discovered she had used a large saucepan, instead of a preserving pan, and because I hadn't said otherwise in the recipe, she had kept the lid on! Don't let the lack of a preserving pan stop you from making jams and pickles, but don't ever put the lid on your saucepan.

Jars Ideally, preserving jars are what you need to make life simple, since they seal down with their own proper lids, and can be bought in a variety of sizes. But for economy, if you get into the habit of saving up all the jars that come into your possession, you'll soon build up quite a collection. At the time of writing most of these are of 1 lb (450 g) capacity, which works well for most things (except pickled onions), so I have kept to this size as a guideline in most recipes. But it's really not important—other sizes of jar can be used; if each one is filled to capacity, then any left-overs can be stored in small jars or used up quickly. You must bear in mind that the vinegar in pickles and chutneys can corrode metal, so for these plastic coated lids are essential. *Warning:* never use paper or cellophane covers for pickles and chutneys. They are fine for jams, but vinegar will evaporate during long storage if the jars aren't completely airtight (which paper covers never are). This is why chutney shrinks and dries out when covered with paper.

All jars and lids for preserving must be washed in warm, soapy water, rinsed thoroughly in warm water, then well dried with a clean towel. As an extra precaution I always place the jars in a moderate oven for 5 minutes, and pour the contents in while the jars are very hot. If you want to use a jar that once contained pickled onions for something else, soak it overnight in cold water with a teaspoonful of bicarbonate of soda stirred in. This should remove any evidence of pickled onions by the next day!

Gauze In my early days of cooking I used to get infuriated when cookery books demanded muslin bags to hold the spices, because I never had such a thing as muslin lying around. However I then discovered that ordinary gauze from the chemist was perfect for the job of holding spices for pickles (or pips for jam-making).

Waxed paper discs Circles of waxed paper are placed over chutneys and jams (wax-side down) to provide a seal. These can be made from the waxed paper found in breakfast cereal packets, or bought from stationers ready-made.

Ingredients for preserving
The vital point to remember is that all ingredients like fruit and vegetables for preserving must be sound. Anything that looks damaged or decayed in the slightest way should not be used.

Chutney-making

Chutney is derived from a Hindu word, and in fact reveals the origin of this particular form of preserving—namely India. In the first place, chutneys were attempts to reproduce in Britain the exotic recipes brought back by our Indian traders in the 18th and 19th centuries: but these efforts very soon brought forth a large range of home-grown preserves—of which piccalilli is one of the best-known examples. Our own native fruits, like plums, damsons and unripe tomatoes, proved excellent for this form of preserving, which is basically simmering slowly in vinegar.

A chutney is ready when the vinegar has reduced sufficiently. The way to tell this is to make a channel with a wooden spoon right across the surface of the chutney. If the spoon leaves a channel imprinted for a few seconds—without it being filled with vinegar—then the chutney is ready.

All chutneys should be stored for at least three months before using. This causes them to mature and mellow in flavour (a really freshly-made chutney, if you were to taste it, would be too harsh and vinegary). A cool, dark place is usually recommended for storage, and in these days of central heating I have found under the bed in the spare bedroom as good a place as any! Failing that, a covered cardboard box in the garage or garden shed will do.

Green tomato chutney

(makes about 8 lb or 3·65 kg)

Originally I thought this was a good recipe for using up all those stubborn green tomatoes that never seemed to ripen, but now we all love this chutney so much I don't even want half my tomatoes to ripen—just so I'll be able to make plenty.

2½ lb green tomatoes (1 kg)
2½ lb cooking apples (1 kg)
2 lb onions (900 g)
6 large cloves garlic, crushed
1 lb raisins (450 g)
1 lb 6 oz soft brown sugar (or demerara) (625 g)
1 oz pickling spice (25 g)
½ tablespoon cayenne pepper
2 level dessertspoons ground ginger

½ tablespoon salt
3 pints genuine malt vinegar (1·75 litres)

A small preserving pan, 8 × 1 lb (450 g) preserving jars, a mincer, string and some gauze

Wash the tomatoes and cut them into quarters, peel the onions and quarter them and likewise with the apples, coring them as well and keeping in water to prevent browning.

Using the medium blade of the mincer, mince the tomatoes and place them in the pan, next the onions, then the raisins followed by the apples (don't worry if they have turned brown). Now add the garlic, the cayenne, salt, ginger and sugar, blending everything thoroughly. Next tie the pickling spice in a small piece of double-thickness gauze and attach it to the handle so that it hangs down into the other ingredients. Now pour in the vinegar, bring to simmering point, remove any scum from the surface, then let it simmer very gently for about 3½ hours without covering. Stir now and then, especially towards the end, to prevent sticking. It's ready when the vinegar has been almost absorbed and the chutney has thickened to a nice soft consistency and the spoon leaves a trail. Do be careful not to overcook, and remember it does thicken up quite a bit as it cools.

Pour the hot chutney into hot jars, filling them as full as possible. Cover with waxed sealing discs and seal with a tight lid at once. Label the jars when the chutney is cold.

Spiced plum chutney

(makes about 6 lb or 2·75 kg)

When the preserving season comes around, this plum chutney is an automatic choice with us. You can also make it with damsons, stewed in their own juice to remove the stones.

3 lb plums (1·35 kg), the small dark ones are best
3 largish onions
1 lb cooking apples (450 g)
1 lb seedless raisins (450 g)
1 lb dark soft brown sugar (450 g)

1 lb demerara sugar (450 g)
1 dessertspoon whole cloves
2 pints malt vinegar (1·25 litres)
3 cloves garlic
2 heaped teaspoons ground ginger
2 tablespoons salt
2 small cinnamon sticks
1 oz whole allspice berries (25 g)

A preserving pan (or very large pan), a 12 inch (30 cm) square piece of gauze (which can be bought from chemists), some string and 6 × 1 lb (450 g) preserving (Kilner) jars or jars with plastic-lined screw-top lids

First of all wash and dry the plums, then slit them down the natural line of the fruit with a sharp knife and remove the stones—putting the halved plums into the pan as you go. Next peel, core and mince the apples and add them to the pan, and do the same with the onions.

Now crush the garlic and add that, followed by the ginger and raisins, the sugars and the vinegar. Sprinkle in the salt and stir everything thoroughly. The cinnamon, allspice berries and cloves should be wrapped in the gauze and tied loosely to form a little bag, which should then be tied onto the handle of the pan and suspended into the middle of the rest of the ingredients.

Bring everything to the boil, then lower the heat and let the chutney simmer very gently for 2–3 hours, stirring it occasionally and rather more often towards the end to prevent it sticking to the bottom. When almost all the vinegar has disappeared and the chutney has thickened to a soft consistency, it's ready. It *will* thicken more when it has cooled, so be careful not to overcook it (and remember the narrower the top of the pan the longer the chutney will take to reduce).

While it is still warm, pour it into the jars (washed, dried and put into a moderate oven to warm through first). Cover with waxed discs and seal down with a screw lid—not paper and string because vinegar will evaporate during storing and the chutney will shrink and dry out. Label when cold and store in a cool, airy cupboard. Leave to mellow for at least three months before eating.

Old Doverhouse chutney

(makes 8 lb, 3·65 kg)

This is a very old recipe handed to me hand-written on a yellowing page from a cookbook belonging to someone's great-grandmother. Where the name came from I've no idea but the chutney is delicious.

1½ lb plums, preferably Victorias (700 g)
1½ lb cooking apples, weighed after peeling (700 g)—about 2 lb (900 g) to start with
8 oz green or red tomatoes (225 g), whatever's available
1 lb stoned raisins (450 g)
8 oz onions (225 g)
1½ lb demerara sugar (700 g)
4 oz preserved ginger (110 g)—the sort that's preserved in syrup
¼ oz garlic, finely chopped (5 g)
¼ oz whole chillies (5 g)
1½ tablespoons cooking salt
1 pint malt vinegar (570 ml)

A preserving pan or very large saucepan, a small square of gauze, and some string. Eight 1 lb (450 g) jars.

First, pick over the plums and wash them, then cut them in half, remove the stones and cut the halves into two (or if very large into three). Then chop the tomatoes roughly into not-too-small pieces, and place both plums and tomatoes into a preserving pan.

Now pass the onions, apples, raisins and preserved ginger through the coarse blade of a mincer, or chop them finely in a food processor, and add these to the pan together with the chopped garlic, vinegar, sugar and salt. Tie the chillies in the gauze with string and suspend them from the handle of the pan. Now cook the chutney very slowly for about 1–1½ hours, or until most of the liquid has evaporated and you've given it the 'channel' test as described on page 660. Also, have a few good stirs during the cooking—and especially towards the end to prevent the mixture sticking to the base of the pan. Pot the chutney when it is still hot into hot jars. Seal with waxed discs and tight lids. Label the jars when the chutney is cold.

Sweet piccalilli

(makes about 5 lb or 2·25 kg)

There's nothing like a few home-made pickles and chutneys for brightening up left-over meat, sausages or other winter economy dishes. When there are no runner beans left, this one can be made with frozen string beans (sometimes called *haricots verts*).

1 lb runner beans (450 g), cut into largish slices for cooking
2 medium-sized cauliflowers, divided into 1 inch (2·5 cm) florets
1 lb small onions (450 g), quartered and cut across
2 cloves garlic, crushed with 3 teaspoons salt
1 cucumber, peeled, cut into ¼ inch (½ cm) rounds, then each round quartered
2 pints malt vinegar (1·25 litres)
12 oz caster sugar (350 g)
2 oz English mustard powder (50 g)
6 tablespoons plain flour
1 oz turmeric powder (25 g)
Half a whole nutmeg, grated
½ teaspoon powdered allspice
5 additional tablespoons malt vinegar
3 tablespoons water

5 × 1 lb jars (450 g)

First place the cauliflower florets, onions and vinegar together in a large saucepan, then add the nutmeg and allspice and bring to the boil. Cover and simmer for 8 minutes. Now take the lid off and stir in the cucumber, runner beans and sugar. Crush the garlic in the salt and stir this in as well. Bring the mixture up to simmering point again, cover and cook for a further 5 minutes. The vegetables should still all be slightly crisp—so don't go away and forget them.

Now set a large colander over a large bowl and pour the contents of the saucepan into it and leave it all to drain (reserving the vinegar). Then mix the mustard powder, turmeric and flour together in a bowl. Gradually work in 5 additional tablespoons of vinegar and 3 of water so that the mixture becomes a fairly loose paste. Next add a ladleful of the hot vinegar liquid, drained from the vegetables, stir and transfer the blend to a saucepan.

Bring to the boil, whisking with a balloon whisk, and gradually adding the remaining hot vinegar. Boil gently for 5 minutes, then transfer the vegetables from the colander to the large bowl, and pour over the sauce. Stir well to mix, then spoon the piccalilli into heated, warmed and dried screw-top jars. Keep for three months before eating.

Note: if you get lumps in the sauce, whisk with a rotary whisk to disperse them.

Victoria plum or damson ketchup
(makes 3½ pints or 2 litres)

This is delicious served with cold meats or sausages and will keep indefinitely. Use bottles that have contained shop-bought ketchup or you can buy the old-fashioned type 'pop' bottles from good kitchen shops.

8 lb plums or damsons (3 kg 600 g)
8 oz currants (225 g)
1 lb onions, chopped small (450 g)
2 oz coarse salt, grated (50 g)
1 lb demerara sugar (450 g)
2 pints distilled white vinegar (1·25 litres)

Tie the following spices in a piece of gauze:
6–8 dried chillies
1 tablespoon black peppercorns
1 tablespoon mustard seeds
½ oz dried root ginger, crushed a bit first (10 g)
½ oz allspice berries (10 g)
2 whole garlic cloves

First slit the plums with a sharp knife and remove the stones, then place the fruit in a large pan and add the currants, onions and the bag of spices. Add 1 pint (570 ml) of the vinegar, bring to the boil and simmer gently, uncovered, for about 30 minutes or until the mixture is soft.

Now remove the bag of spices, place the contents of the pan in a liquidiser and blend until perfectly smooth—if necessary sieve as well. Then rinse out the pan and return the purée and bag of spices to it, adding the salt, sugar and the remaining 1 pint (570 ml) of vinegar. Bring to simmering point and cook gently, uncovered, for 1½–2 hours or until the ketchup has reduced to approximately 3½ pints (2 litres). Stir now and then to prevent sticking.

In the meantime prepare the containers by boiling the bottles and their tops. When the ketchup is ready pour it into the bottles while they're still hot, filling them to within an inch (2·5 cm) of the top. Put on the tops immediately but screw them only half-way and if you're using the 'pop' type bottles push the top in but leave the lever up.

Next place the bottles in a pan (standing them on an upside down plate) and add warm water to within 1½ inches (4 cm) from the tops. Bring the water to the boil and after 10 minutes transfer the bottles to a wooden surface and complete the sealing.

Note: although it has never happened to me, I have heard of the upside down plate sometimes breaking—so perhaps an enamel plate would be safer.

Cranberry and orange relish

(serves 8 people)

This cranberry sauce is an excellent accompaniment to the Christmas turkey, but there is no need to confine it to that: it goes just as well with many poultry, pork or ham dishes too.

1 lb fresh cranberries (450 g)
The zest and juice of 1 orange
Piece of cinnamon stick
3 oz sugar (75 g)
4 cloves
½ teaspoon ginger
2 tablespoons port

Begin by mincing the cranberries finely, then put them into a saucepan. Remove the outer zest of the orange (with a potato peeler if you like) and cut into very thin strips. Now add these strips of zest together with the juice of the orange to the minced cranberries, followed by the cinnamon stick, cloves, ginger and the sugar. Bring the whole lot to boiling point, put a lid on and cook gently for about 5 minutes. Then take the pan off the heat and stir in the port. Pour everything into a serving bowl, cover it and leave in the refrigerator until required (remembering to remove the cinnamon and cloves before serving).

Pickling

I'm afraid I have neither the stamina nor the patience to endure long pickling sessions (especially with onions). So I always use the method in the recipe below, which cuts out the normal salting and brining process. The results are excellent, except that the vegetables pickled in this way do need to be eaten within three or four months. I actually find that no hardship—a batch made in October ensures a good supply for Christmas, and after that another batch can be made. The whole thing takes about 45 minutes from start to finish. (For those who require longer-keeping pickles, may I refer you to the specialised books on preserving in the book list, page 707).

Quick pickled onions

In this recipe I put the spices in with the onions, which gives them a lovely, hot spicy flavour. Just the thing to serve with strong Cheddar cheese, real bread and real ale.

4¾ lb pickling onions (2 kg 150 g)
3¼ pints malt vinegar (1 litre 850 ml)
1 oz pickling spice (25 g)

4 × 1¾ pint (1 litre) preserving jars (or the equivalent)

Peel the onions—preferably while you listen to some good music on the radio to take your mind off the job. Then pack the jars half-full with the onions and sprinkle a level dessertspoon of pickling spice into each jar. Then fill up each jar with more onions, followed by another dessertspoon of pickling spice.

Now pour the vinegar over the onions, right up to the top so that it covers them completely, and fix on the lids. Store in a cool, dark place for at least 8 weeks before eating.

Note: if you don't have proper preserving jars, any other jars will do, provided they have plastic-coated lids. Paper covers will *not* do—see notes on jars, page 659.

Pickled red cabbage

This, again, is made by the quick no-salting method; and the cabbage keeps perfectly crisp for up to four months.

1½ lb red cabbage, cleaned and shredded (700 g)
1¾ pints malt vinegar (1 l)
1 oz pickling spice (25 g)
1 level tablespoon coriander seeds

5 × 1 lb (450 g) preserving jars, washed and dried

Place the pickling spice in a saucepan with the vinegar, cover with a lid, and bring to simmering point very slowly over a gentle heat. Then remove the pan from the heat, and allow the vinegar to infuse the spicy flavours for about 4 hours.

After that strain the vinegar into a large mixing bowl (reserving the spices), stir in the red cabbage and the coriander seeds, and mix thoroughly. Now spoon this mixture into the prepared jars, making sure each jar has enough vinegar to come right up to the top. Extract some pieces of red chilli (or whole ones) from the pickling spices, and place them amongst the red cabbage. Seal down the jars and store for about 2 months before opening.

Jam and marmalade making

The great advantage of home-made jams is that they are pure, made from fruit and sugar only—unlike their shop-bought cousins which often list several other ingredients as well. It is true you *can* buy the more expensive brands which proudly display the fact that they contain no preservative or colouring, but (being an avid jam label studier) I have rarely come across a jam—or a marmalade —that is made only from fruit and sugar, whatever the price. The answer, both in terms of quality and economy, is to make them at home and add a touch of luxury to everyday eating.

What is jam? Essentially it's preserved fruit. The fruit, if it is in good condition and slightly under-ripe, contains in its cell walls a natural setting agent called pectin. This, together with the natural acid from the fruit, is released when the fruit is boiled with sugar. As the mixture boils, the sugar concentrates and all three (sugar, acid and pectin) combine to form a mass that eventually reaches 'setting point'.

Ingredients
Fruit First of all, this should be dry since the water content in damp fruit will dilute the pectin and the acid, and render them less active. Very dusty fruit should be wiped with damp kitchen paper, but normally the boiling process will effectively purify the fruit. Research has shown that slightly under-ripe fruit contains a lot more pectin and fruit acid than over-ripe fruit (which should be avoided). With those fruits that contain less acid than others, this deficiency is made up by adding lemon juice.

Sugar The proportion of sugar to fruit varies according to the type of fruit used. For me, the really sharp fruits—like damsons or loganberries—make the best jams because they are not over-powered by the sweetness of the sugar. In other words, the fruit flavour is stronger. This is also why I believe the bitter Seville oranges make the best marmalade: tasting of oranges rather than sugar. I don't find that special preserving sugar is essential, and in fact never use it because it's so much more expensive.

Equipment
The equipment for jam-making is the same as that outlined at the beginning of the chapter, except you will find some recipes advise the use of jam thermometers. These are clipped to the side of the preserving pan, and when the mixture reaches 220°F (104°C) setting point should be reached. However I must say I have never had much success with thermometers, perhaps because the steam caused by fast-boiling makes it impossible to see the temperature clearly (and if you take the thermometer out, the temperature marking drops immediately). I would recommend you use the 'cold plate' test, see page 670.

Jars They need the same treatment as outlined on page 659, except that in this case the coverings can be cellophane discs kept in place by elastic bands. These are sold in packets, which also contain the waxed discs. Many people say cellophane is the best covering, though it must be admitted that proper lids are a lot more convenient when you start to eat the jam!

Important points for jam-making
(1) Tough-skinned fruits should be simmered and softened before the sugar is added, as the sugar has a hardening effect.
(2) Soft-skinned fruits (like strawberries) that tend to disintegrate when cooked should be soaked in sugar first to harden them—and

so help to keep the fruit in the finished jam whole.

(3) The sugar must be dissolved completely before the jam is boiled, otherwise it will be difficult to set and the finished jam will be sugary. To test if the sugar has dissolved, dip a wooden spoon in, turn it over, and if no sugar crystals are visible on the liquid that coats the spoon, it has indeed dissolved. (But be sure to stir well and try this test two or three times.) To speed up the dissolving process, you can warm the sugar in a bowl in the oven before adding it.

(4) Never try to make jam in too large quantities. It will take far too long to come to the boil, and then will not boil rapidly enough to produce a good set.

(5) *How to test for a set:* when you start to cook the fruit place about four small plates in the freezing compartment of the fridge. Then, when you have boiled the jam for the given time, remove the pan from the heat, and place a teaspoonful of the jam onto one of the chilled plates. Allow it to cool for a few seconds, then push it with your finger: if a crinkly skin has formed on the jam, then it has set. If it hasn't set, boil it again for another 5 minutes and then do another test.

(6) Ignore any scum that rises to the surface while the jam is boiling. If you keep skimming it off, you'll find you have no jam left! Instead, wait until you have a set, then remove the jam from the heat and stir in a small lump of butter which will disperse the scum.

(7) After the jam has set, allow it to settle for 15 minutes (especially necessary for jam containing whole fruit—such as strawberry or damson or even chunky marmalade—to prevent the fruit rising to the top when it's poured into the jar). Then pour into dry, clean, warmed jars, filling them as far up to the neck as possible. Then immediately place a waxed disc over the surface, and tie down straightaway with cellophane covering (to do this, wipe the cellophane with a damp cloth and place it on the jar damp side up). Wipe the jars with a hot damp cloth.

(8) Don't put the labels on until the jam is cold, since the heat will prevent them sticking properly and they will very soon peel off.

(9) Store in a cool, dry, and preferably dark, place. Too much light is not good for storage, while a damp or steamy atmosphere can cause mould to develop on the surface of your jam.

(10) If things go wrong. . . . If the jam hasn't set after cooling and potting, tip it all back into the pan and boil again adding the juice of a small lemon. If a mould develops on the surface, remove it

plus about half an inch of the jam underneath. The rest of the jam will not be affected.

(11) There is no need to use commercially produced pectin. It's expensive and shouldn't ever be necessary.

Strawberry jam

(makes 6 lb or 2·75 kg)

The way to keep strawberries whole in jam is to cover them with the sugar and leave them overnight. The sugar draws out the juices and firms the fruit.

4 lb slightly under-ripe dry strawberries (2 kg)
3 lb sugar (1·35 kg)
The juice of 2 large lemons

A preserving pan with a lightly buttered base

4 small plates chilled in the ice-making compartment of the refrigerator

Hull the strawberries and wipe with some damp kitchen paper, then layer them in the preserving pan, sprinkling them with the sugar as you go. Leave them like this overnight, by which time the sugar should have almost dissolved.

To make the jam, place the pan over a lowish heat just to melt the rest of the sugar and draw some of the juice out of the strawberries—don't stir too much, just shake the pan now and then to keep the fruit as whole as possible. When the sugar has completely dissolved, add the lemon juice, turn up the heat and as soon as the jam is really bubbling, time it for 8 minutes and then remove it from the heat. Spoon a little onto a chilled plate, allow it to cool, then push with your little finger: if it forms a crinkly skin, it's set. If not, boil it up for a further 3–4 minutes. Repeat the test, removing the pan from the heat three or four times if necessary until you have a set.

Then remove from the heat, stir in a small lump of butter to disperse any scum, and allow the jam to settle for 15 minutes before pouring it into dry clean jars (heated in a moderate oven for 5 minutes). Seal immediately with waxed discs and tie down while still warm. Label when cold.

Note: try not to wash strawberries or attempt to make jam after it has rained heavily and the fruit is wet—it must be as dry as possible. If you are forced to wash the fruit, dry it and spread it out on clean teacloths to dry further before using. Any extra moisture will dilute the pectin and make setting more difficult.

Loganberry jam

(makes 5 lb or 2·25 kg)

You can make this in any quantity using 1 lb (450 g) of sugar for each pound of loganberries.

3 lb loganberries, preferably under-ripe (1 kg 350 g)

3 lb granulated sugar (1 kg 350 g)

Pre-heat the oven to gas mark 4, 350°F (180°C)

5 × 1 lb (450 g) jars, washed, dried and heated in a moderate oven for 5 minutes

Put 4 small plates into the freezer compartment of the fridge to get them really cold

Pick over the fruit, discarding any stalks or leafy bits, then put them into a pan. Don't wash them as the heat from the cooking will purify them. Place the pan on a fairly low heat—don't stir at all, just leave it on the heat until the juices start to run.

Then, gently, shake the pan from side to side, to get the top loganberries down to the bottom; or you can stir, but be careful and try not to break the fruit too much—it's nice to get some whole fruits in the finished jam. Now leave it to cook very slowly for about 30 minutes or until the fruit is cooked and all the berries are tender.

While all that's happening—in fact as soon as you've put the fruit on to cook—tip the sugar into a bowl and place it in the pre-heated oven. When the fruit is cooked, add the hot sugar, tipping the pan and stirring gently. Then leave it again on a low heat for a further 15 minutes or so until the sugar has dissolved completely—it's very important no sugar crystals should be left or the finished jam will go sugary. The way to test this is by coating the back of a wooden spoon with the mixture and you will be able to see if the sugar hasn't dissolved.

As soon as it has dissolved, turn the heat right up as high as it will go, and boil the jam rapidly for 10 minutes. Then remove it from the heat, spoon a little onto one of your cooled plates, and when it's cool push the jam with your little finger. If a crinkly skin has formed, it's set. If not boil it rapidly again for 5 minutes, test again and carry on like this until the jam has set.

Ignore any scum while the jam is boiling, but as soon as it's set, add a little knob of butter which will get rid of most of it (you can skim off any that's left with a slotted spoon). Leave the jam for 15 minutes to settle, then pour it into the hot jars, filling them right to the top. Cover straight away with waxed discs, and seal with tight-fitting lids or cellophane. Label the jars when the jam is cold.

Note: always store preserves in a cool, dark, airy cupboard.

Other varieties of jam
Damson jam
Use 2¼ lb (1 kg 60 g) of sugar to 3 lb (1 kg 350g) of fruit. Simmer the fruit in ¾ pint (425 ml) of water until soft, then proceed as for *Loganberry jam* on the previous page.

Plum jam
Use 2 lb (900 g) stoned, halved fruit and 1½ lb (700 g) sugar. Simmer the fruit in 8 fl oz of water until tender, then proceed as for *Loganberry jam*.

Blackcurrant jam
Use 2 lb (900 g) of fruit simmered in 1 pint (570 ml) of water until tender. Add 2½ lb (1 kg 125 g) of sugar and continue as for *Loganberry jam*.

Seville orange marmalade
(makes 6 lb or 2·75 kg)

The ingredients below make 6 lb (2 kg 750 g). I find it harder to make larger quantities in one go.

| 2 lb Seville oranges (900 g) |
| 1 lemon |
| 4 lb granulated sugar, warmed (1·8 kg) |
| 4 pints water (2·25 litres) |

6 × 1 lb (450 g) jars, 9 inch (23 cm)
square of gauze, string

Begin by measuring the water into a preserving pan, then cut the lemon and oranges in half and squeeze the juice out of them. Add the juice to the water, and place the pips and any bits of pith that cling to the squeezer on the square of muslin (laid over a dish or cereal bowl first). Now cut the orange peel into quarters with a sharp knife, and then cut each quarter into thinnish shreds. As you cut add the shreds to the water and any pips or spare pith you come across should go onto the muslin. Remember that the pith contains a lot of pectin so don't discard any.

Now tie the pips up loosely in the muslin to form a little bag, and tie this onto the handle of the pan so that the bag is suspended in the water. Then bring the liquid up to simmering point, and simmer gently, uncovered, for 2 hours or thereabouts until the peel is completely soft—test a piece carefully by pressing it between your finger and thumb. At this point pop three or four tea-plates into the freezing compartment of the fridge.

Next remove the bag of pips and leave it to cool on a saucer. Then pour the sugar into the pan and stir it now and then over a low heat, until all the crystals have melted (check this carefully, it's important). Now increase the heat to very high, and squeeze the bag of pips over the pan to extract all of the sticky, jelly-like substance that contains the pectin. As you squeeze you'll see it ooze out. You can do this by placing the bag between two saucers or, if you're impatient like me, use your hands. Then stir or whisk it into the rest.

As soon as the mixture reaches a really fast boil, start timing. Then after 15 minutes spoon a little of the marmalade onto one of the cold plates from the fridge, and let it cool back in the fridge. You can tell—when it has cooled—if you have a 'set' by pushing the mixture with your little finger: if it has a really crinkly skin, it is set. If not, continue to boil the marmalade and give it the same test at about 10-minute intervals until it does set.

After that remove the pan from the heat (if there's a lot of scum, most of it can be dispersed by stirring in half a teaspoon of butter, and the rest can be spooned off). Leave the marmalade to settle for 20 minutes.

In the meantime the jars (washed, rinsed and dried first) should be heated in a moderate oven for 5 minutes. Pour the marmalade, with the aid of a funnel or a ladle, into the jars and cover with waxed discs and seal while still hot. Label the jars when quite cold.

Quick bramble jelly

(makes 1 lb or 450 g)

This is not a jelly that will keep for long—perhaps only a month—but if you've been for a long walk in the autumn and returned with a harvest of brambles from the hedgerows, this recipe is so easy and quick to make and it does taste delicious spread on hot crumpets or scones.

1 lb ripe blackberries (450 g)
1 lb granulated sugar (450 g)
6 fl oz water (170 ml)
Juice of 1 lemon

A large nylon sieve and a piece of chemist's gauze about 14 inches (35 cm) square

Wash the blackberries and place in a thick-based saucepan with the water, then stew them very gently with a lid on for about 20–25 minutes. Now and then give them a good mash to reduce them to pulp and squeeze as much juice out of them as possible. After that add the sugar and lemon juice to the pan and allow the sugar to dissolve completely, with the heat still low. There must not be any whole granules of sugar left. This takes about 10–15 minutes. Now turn the heat right up and boil fairly rapidly for 8 minutes, stirring now and then to prevent sticking.

Meanwhile warm a large bowl and a 1 lb (450 g) jam jar in the oven—get them nice and hot—and then place the sieve, lined with gauze, over the bowl and pour the blackberry mixture into the lined sieve. Then, using a wooden spoon, get all the liquid through as quickly as possible, squeezing the remaining pulp as much as you can—but do be quick as the jelly sets if you take too long. Now pour the jelly into the warmed jar, cover with a waxed disc, cool and tie down.

Note: if it begins to set before you've had a chance to pour it into the jar, just re-heat it gently again.

Redcurrant jelly

(makes 2 lb or 900 g)

One preserve that has suffered bitterly from commercialism is redcurrant jelly: so often it is sickly sweet and the flavour of the redcurrants is lost amongst other ingredients. Luckily I've found an extremely easy recipe for making it from Eliza Acton's *Modern Cookery for Private Families* (1840). Her name for it was 'Superlative Redcurrant Jelly'.

---

2 lb redcurrants (900 g)

2 lb sugar (900 g), warmed

---

1 packet gauze from the chemists, 1 large nylon sieve, 2 × 1 lb (450 g) jars, washed, dried and heated in a moderate oven for 5 minutes

The first easy thing is that there's no need to go through the tedious business of stripping the currants from the stalks. Just place the washed fruit—stalks and all—in a preserving pan, bring slowly to the boil, and stir and press the redcurrants to break down the fruit and release the juice. As soon as the fruit is cooked (about 10 minutes), add the warmed sugar, stir until absolutely dissolved, then bring the mixture up to a rapid boil, and boil for 8 minutes.

Meanwhile place a large nylon sieve over a bowl and line it with a double layer of gauze. Then, when the 8 minutes are up, tip the whole lot into the sieve and let it drip through. If you don't mind not having a completely clear jelly, you can press to extract as much as possible. Then pour the jelly into warmed jars, cover with waxed discs and tie down.

Note: this makes 2 lb (900 g), but the process is exactly the same for a larger quantity.

Home-made Christmas mincemeat

(makes 6 lb or 2·75 kg)

I give you a warning here. Once you've tasted home-made mincemeat in mince pies, you'll never again be able to revert to shop-bought!

---

1 lb cooking apples, peeled, cored and finely chopped (450 g)

8 oz shredded suet (225 g)
12 oz raisins (350 g)
8 oz sultanas (225 g)
8 oz currants (225 g)
8 oz whole mixed peel, finely chopped (225 g)
12 oz soft dark brown sugar (350 g)
The grated rind and juice of 2 oranges
The grated rind and juice of 2 lemons
2 oz whole almonds, cut into slivers (50 g)
4 teaspoons mixed spice
½ teaspoon ground cinnamon
Half a nutmeg, grated
6 tablespoons brandy

Just mix all the ingredients, except for the brandy, together in a large bowl very thoroughly. Then cover with a cloth and leave for 12 hours. To prevent fermentation place the mincemeat in a cool oven, gas mark ¼, 225°F (120°C) for 3 hours. Then allow it to get quite cold, stir in the brandy and spoon into clean dry jars. Cover with waxed discs, then seal.

Uncle Billy's toffee

(makes about 1¼ lb or 575 g)

For years my Uncle Billy (from Wales) cherished the secret of his home-made toffee—which is the best I've ever tasted, I swear. Now he has relented, and I can pass on to you the recipe for this buttery, chewy delicacy!

1 lb soft brown sugar (450 g)
12 oz salted butter (350 g)
1 teaspoon malt vinegar
5 fl oz water (150 ml)

A shallow tin 7½ inch (19 cm) square, lightly oiled

First take your very largest saucepan—toffee tends to boil over if it doesn't have much room, so a 4½ or 5 pint (2·5 or 3 litre) one would be ideal. Put all the ingredients in the saucepan, and bring them *slowly* to the boil over a low heat (about 10–15 minutes), stirring occasionally. When the sugar has completely dissolved, turn the heat up a little, insert a cooking thermometer and let the mixture bubble away (without stirring) until the temperature reaches 250°F (130°C)—which will take about 10 minutes. Then pour it into the prepared tin and leave to set.

When it has set, turn the toffee out onto a board and break it up with a small hammer (or other heavy object), then store the pieces in a polythene bag tied at the neck.

Note: if you do not possess a cooking thermometer, test the toffee by dropping a teaspoonful into a saucer of cold water: if it sets immediately into a soft, pliable ball, the toffee is ready.

Fruits and cold puddings

Including recipes for:

If this chapter seems at variance with my continuing war on sugar consumption, let me say I am all in favour of delicious puddings and sweet dishes—but *not* too often. I happen neither to eat sweets and confectionery nor drink soft drinks, but I do think a really mouth-watering cake or pudding is something to be enjoyed on all feast days and holidays. Very often sweet recipes contain what I would consider an excessive amount of sugar, but even in this chapter you won't find anything with low calories or artificial sweeteners (or any other type of slimmers' aid). So having made the point, let's consider some of the ingredients that will be used.

Gelatine Cold mousses, soufflés and jellies need flavourless gelatine to get them to set. One detail worth paying close attention to is to make sure your gelatine has dissolved properly: failure to do so is perhaps the commonest cause of problems.

  There are two kinds of gelatine. One (not very widely available) is transparent leaf gelatine. The other is powdered gelatine, which comes in packets of $\frac{1}{2}$ oz (10 g) each. This amount of powdered gelatine is usually enough to stiffen 1 pint (570 ml) of liquid (or use three sheets of gelatine per pint).

  The best way to dissolve gelatine is to sprinkle it into a cup or small basin containing 3–4 tablespoons of some hot or cold liquid. Stir it, and when the gelatine has soaked up the liquid place the cup in a pan of barely simmering water and leave until it has dissolved completely and turned transparent. To test this, dip a teaspoon in it, turn it over and you'll soon see if there are any undissolved granules. It's important not to let the liquid boil—so keep the heat under the pan gentle, and before you use it pass the gelatine through a strainer, to extract any bits of skin that may have formed. Another tip (that appears on the back of some packets) is that you should sprinkle the gelatine granules onto the liquid, and not the other way round.

Cream Only double cream (or whipping cream) is suitable for whipping. Take care, though, because over-whisking can cause the cream to take on a curdled appearance, so that it won't fold into anything nor go through a piping bag. So if you have to fold cream into anything, beat it only to the thickened 'floppy' stage. For piping it has to be stiffer: beat it until stiff peaks are left when you lift the whisk from the cream (but again, don't overdo it).

Chocolate Melting chocolate can be a tricky affair. Overheating, or leaving it near the heat too long, makes it granular when other ingredients are added, and the chocolate loses all its gloss. But if you deal with it carefully you'll never have any problems. Just break the chocolate up into small squares, place them in a basin fitted over a pan of barely simmering water (if it's boiling too fast turn the heat out, so that you just have very hot water), and the chocolate will soon start to melt round the edge. Then stir it with a wooden spoon, and in 3–5 minutes it will all have melted and become smoothly liquid.

Summer pudding

(serves 6 people)

Maybe the reason why this pudding is such a favourite is because we only have these particular fruits for a short time each year—anyway in our house it's become a sort of annual event.

1 lb raspberries (450 g)
8 oz redcurrants (225 g)
4 oz blackcurrants (110 g)
5 oz caster sugar (150 g)
7–8 medium slices white bread from a large loaf

A 1½ pint (850 ml) pudding basin, lightly buttered

First of all the fruit must be prepared. Separate the redcurrants and blackcurrants from their stalks by holding the tip of each stalk firmly between finger and thumb and sliding it between the prongs of a fork—pushing the fork downwards, so pulling off the berries as it goes. Rinse all the fruits, picking out any raspberries that look at all musty.

Place the fruits with the sugar in a large saucepan over a medium heat and let them cook for about 3–5 minutes, only until the sugar has melted and the juices begin to run—don't overcook and so spoil the fresh flavour. Now remove the fruit from the heat, and line a 1½ pint (850 ml) pudding basin with the slices of bread, overlapping them and sealing well by pressing the edges together. Fill in any gaps with small pieces of bread, so that no juice can get through when you add the fruit.

Pour the fruit in (except for a cupful of juice), and cover the pudding with another slice of bread. Then place a small plate or saucer (one that will fit exactly inside the rim of the bowl) on top, and on top of that place a 3 lb or 4 lb (1·4 kg or 1·8 kg) weight, and leave in the refrigerator overnight.

Just before serving the pudding, turn it out on to a large serving dish and spoon the reserved juice all over, to soak any bits of bread that still look white. Serve cut into slices, with a bowl of thick cream on the table.

Pavlova
(serves 6 people)

This is a delicious pudding from New Zealand, which is very difficult to make if you don't have the right recipe but dead easy if you do!

3 large fresh egg whites
6 oz caster sugar (175 g)
½ pint whipped cream (275 ml)
12 oz soft fruits (350 g)—raspberries, strawberries and redcurrants mixed
A little icing sugar

Pre-heat the oven to gas mark 2, 300°F (150°C)

A lightly-oiled baking sheet, lined with greaseproof paper (which should also be oiled lightly) or silicone paper which peels off very easily

Place the egg whites in a large clean bowl and have the sugar measured and ready. Now whisk the egg whites until they form soft peaks and you can turn the bowl upside down without them sliding out (it's very important, though, not to over-beat the eggs because, if you do, they will start to collapse).

When they're ready, start to whisk in the sugar, approximately 1 oz (25 g) at a time, whisking after each addition until all the sugar is in. Now take a metal tablespoon and spoon the meringue mixture onto the prepared baking sheet, forming a circle of about 8 inches (20 cm) in diameter. Make a round depression in the centre and, using the tip of a skewer, make little swirls in the meringue all round the edge, lifting the skewer up sharply each time to leave tiny peaks.

Now place the baking sheet in the oven, then immediately turn down the heat to gas mark 1, 275°F (140°C) and leave it to cook for 1 hour. Then turn the heat right off but *leave* the Pavlova inside the oven until it's completely cold. I always find it's best to make a Pavlova in the evening and leave it in the turned-off oven overnight to dry out. It's my belief that the secret of successful meringues of any sort is to let them dry out completely, which is what this method does perfectly.

To serve the Pavlova, lift it from the baking sheet, peel off the paper and place it on a serving dish. Then just before serving, spread the whipped cream on top, arrange the strawberries, etc., on top of the cream and dust with a little sifted icing sugar. Serve cut into wedges.

Note: of course, this can be made with just one kind of fruit—for the Pavlova in our cover picture, we used just strawberries. In the winter, when there are no soft fruits available, sliced bananas and chopped preserved ginger make a nice alternative filling.

Strawberries in raspberry purée

(serves 4–6 people)

This is one of the simplest and most delicious sweet dishes I know and proves it's not always necessary to spend hours in the kitchen to make something spectacular.

1 lb firm strawberries (450 g)
8 oz raspberries (225 g)
2½ oz sieved icing sugar (60 g)
3 or 4 macaroon biscuits, crushed
5 fl oz double cream (150 ml), whipped

Hull the strawberries, but don't wash them—just gently wipe them with a piece of damp kitchen paper. The raspberries should then be pressed to a pulp through a nylon sieve, and mixed with the icing sugar. Now arrange the strawberries in a bowl (a glass one would show off the attractive colour of this dish), and sit the bowl on some ice-cubes arranged in the bottom of another bowl.

Mix the raspberry purée into the strawberries, then just before serving, top with the whipped cream and sprinkle all over with the crushed macaroons.

Cardinal peaches
(serves 6 people)

These look and taste stunning served in stemmed glass dishes—a really fresh and fragrant way to end a meal.

6 large, ripe peaches
1½ tablespoons caster sugar
2–3 oz icing sugar (50–75 g)
1 vanilla pod
12 oz fresh raspberries (350 g)
1 tablespoon flaked almonds

First wash the peaches and place them, whole and unpeeled, in a large saucepan. Pour in just enough water to cover them, add the caster sugar and the vanilla pod, bring it up to simmering point, then put a lid on and simmer gently for about 10 minutes. Then drain the peaches, and when they're cold slip the skins off.

Meanwhile sprinkle the raspberries with icing sugar and leave them for 20 minutes. Then press them through a nylon sieve to make a purée. Now place the peaches in a bowl and pour the raspberry purée over. Cover with clingfilm and chill thoroughly for several hours. To serve them, place on one large serving dish or in six individual dishes and sprinkle with flaked almonds.

Fresh fruit salad
(serves 8 people)

Any fresh fruit salad may be varied according to whatever fruits are in season but this one seems to have just the right balance. If you don't have rum—or don't like it—you can replace it with fresh orange juice.

1 pineapple
2 bananas
2 Cox's apples
2 Comice pears
2 oranges
8 oz black grapes (225 g)
For the syrup:
4 oz caster sugar (110 g)
½ pint water (275 ml)

The juice of 1 lemon
6 tablespoons rum

Begin by making the syrup. To do this, place the sugar and water in a small pan, and let the sugar dissolve over a gentle heat. Then bring to the boil and simmer for a minute, remove from the heat and add the lemon juice, then tip into a serving bowl to cool. When cold, add the rum.

Now prepare the fruits: peel the oranges and divide into segments, then add all the segments to the syrup in the bowl, and toss well. Rinse and drain the grapes, then cut each one in half and remove the pips before adding to the syrup. Slice the top off the pineapple and cut away the sides and the base: then slice the pineapple across and cut the slices into segments, and add to the syrup. The apples and pears need to be cored but leave the peel on, and slice directly into the syrup. Leave the bananas to last—they discolour the quickest—and slice straight into the bowl. When all the fruit is in, toss everything well, cover the bowl with clingfilm and chill in the fridge before serving.

Dried fruit jelly
(serves 6 people)

This is cool and light and is good after a rich meal. It goes beautifully served with home-made natural yoghurt.

4 oz dried prunes (110 g)
4 oz dried apricots (110 g)
1 strip of orange peel
Juice of 1 orange
1 small piece cinnamon stick
2 oz sugar (50 g)
1 level tablespoon powdered gelatine

Start this off the night before by putting the dried prunes and apricots to soak in a pint (570 ml) of cold water. Then, when you are ready to make the jelly, pour the fruits (and the water they were soaked in) into a saucepan, adding the sugar, cinnamon and orange peel, and simmer gently for 20 minutes. Next fit a sieve over a bowl, pour the fruits into it and let them drain thoroughly. Then pour the liquid into a measuring jug, and add the orange juice and enough water to make it up to a pint (570 ml). At this stage taste to check there's enough sugar.

Now put 3 tablespoons of the liquid into a small bowl, sprinkle in the gelatine and, when it has absorbed all the liquid, fit the bowl over a saucepan of barely simmering water. Stir now and then, and when the gelatine has dissolved and become transparent, strain it back into the rest of the mixture, mixing it in thoroughly.

Take the stones out of the prunes and chop all the flesh of the fruits roughly and arrange in the base of a 2 pint (1·25 litre) mould. Pour the gelatine mixture over the fruit and leave in a cool place to set.

Apricot hazelnut meringue

(serves 6 people)

A light and delicious—and rather special—sweet. You can buy ready-ground hazelnuts at wholefood shops and delicatessens, or if you're grinding your own, brown them first in the oven (gas mark 4, 350°F (180°C) and grind them in a food processor or liquidiser.

3 large egg whites
6 oz caster sugar (175 g)
3 oz ground hazelnuts (75 g)
½ pint double cream (275 ml)
A few whole toasted hazelnuts

For the filling:
4 oz dried apricots, soaked overnight (110 g)
The juice of 1 small orange
A small strip of orange peel
½ inch cinnamon stick (1 cm)
2 teaspoons arrowroot
1 tablespoon brown sugar

Pre-heat the oven to gas mark 5, 375°F (190°C)

Two 7 inch (18 cm) sandwich tins, lightly oiled and the base lined with silicone or greaseproof paper, also lightly oiled

First whisk the egg whites in a bowl until they form stiff peaks, then whisk in the caster sugar, a little at a time. Then, using a

Right: Profiteroles, page 492.

metal spoon, lightly fold in the ground hazelnuts. Now divide the mixture equally between the two tins and level them out. Bake the meringues on the centre shelf of the oven for 20–30 minutes. Leave them in the tins to cool for 30 minutes before turning out (the surface will look uneven, but don't worry). When they've cooled, loosen round the edges, turn them out onto wire racks and strip off the base papers.

While the meringues are cooking, you can prepare the apricot filling. Drain the soaked apricots in a sieve over a bowl, then transfer the apricots to a small saucepan and add the orange juice, peel, cinnamon and sugar plus 2 tablespoons of the soaking water. Simmer gently for 10–15 minutes until they are tender when tested with a skewer, then remove the cinnamon stick and orange peel. Mix the arrowroot with a little cold water and add this to the apricot mixture, stirring over a fairly low heat, until the mixture has thickened. Then leave it to get quite cold.

To serve the meringue: whip the cream, then carefully spread the cold apricot mixture over one meringue, followed by half the whipped cream. Place the other meringue on top, spread the remaining cream over that and decorate the top with some whole toasted hazelnuts.

Traditional trifle

(serves 6–8 people)

This is a real trifle made with proper custard—a bit extravagant but well worth it.

3 egg yolks
1 pint double cream (570 ml)
1 oz caster sugar (25 g)
1 level teaspoon cornflour
5 trifle sponge cakes
2 oz flaked almonds, lightly toasted (50 g)
Some raspberry jam
2 fl oz sherry (55 ml)
8 oz frozen raspberries (225 g)—no need to defrost
2 small bananas, peeled and sliced thinly

Break the sponge cakes in pieces and spread a little raspberry jam on each piece. Then put them into a large glass bowl, sprinkle the

Left: Rich chocolate mousse, page 690; Cardinal peaches, page 684; Blackcurrant ice cream, page 565.

raspberries and sherry over them, giving everything a good stir to soak up the sherry.

To make the custard, heat ½ pint (275 ml) of the double cream in a small saucepan. Blend the egg yolks, sugar and cornflour together thoroughly in a basin, and when the cream is hot, pour it over the egg mixture, stirring the whole time. Now return the custard to the saucepan and stir over a very low heat until thick, then remove it and allow it to cool. Slice the bananas, sprinkle them in amongst the raspberries and pour the custard over the sponge cakes. Whip up the remaining ½ pint (275 ml) of cream and spread it over the top. Decorate with the flaked almonds. Cover and chill for 3 or 4 hours before serving.

Rich chocolate mousse

(serves 2 people)

This one is definitely amongst my top ten favourite puds. It can be made for any number of people if you remember to use 1 egg and 2 oz (50 g) of chocolate per person.

4 oz plain dessert chocolate (110 g)
2 eggs, separated
1 tablespoon rum (or brandy)
2 heaped teaspoons whipped cream
Grated chocolate and/or chopped, toasted nuts

2 stemmed wine glasses or ramekins

Melt the chocolate as described on page 680. When it is smooth and liquid, remove it from the heat. Beat the egg yolks and add them to the chocolate while it's still hot, beating thoroughly (this cooks the egg yolks slightly).

Now leave the mixture to cool for about 20 minutes. Then beat up the egg whites—not too stiffly, just to the soft peak stage—then fold them into the chocolate mixture. Next spoon the mixture into the glasses, cover each one with foil or clingfilm and chill until firm (about 2 hours).

When you're ready to serve, make a few holes in the top of each mousse (using a small skewer or darning needle) and spoon some rum or brandy over the surface to soak in. Then top with a blob of whipped cream and some grated chocolate or chopped nuts. These are very nice served with langue de chat biscuits.

Note: for a *Chocolate orange mousse* add the grated zest and the juice of half an orange to a 4 oz (110 g) quantity of chocolate at the melting stage.

Cold chocolate orange soufflé

(serves 4–6 people)

I have a weakness for anything 'chocolatey' and this is one of my most favourite chocolate puddings.

7 oz plain chocolate (200 g)
3 whole eggs
2 eggs separated
3 oz caster sugar (75 g)
Grated zest and juice of 1 large orange
2 fl oz water (55 ml)
½ oz powdered gelatine (10 g)
3 fl oz double cream (75 ml), lightly beaten until floppy but not thick

For the decoration:
5 fl oz double cream, whipped (150 ml)
1 tablespoon grated chocolate

Start off by soaking the gelatine in the orange juice in an old cup, then place it in a pan of barely simmering water until it has dissolved and become completely transparent.

While that is happening, place the 2 egg yolks, 3 whole eggs and the sugar in a largish mixing bowl and place this over another pan of barely simmering water. Now, using an electric hand or rotary whisk, whisk until the mixture has become thick and creamy which should be in approximately 10 minutes. Then remove the mixing bowl from the heat and place another bowl over the hot water and break the chocolate into it, add the water and stir until the chocolate has melted and become a smooth liquid. Remove it from the heat, stir in the grated orange zest, and leave it to cool for about 15 minutes. Now stir and fold the chocolate mixture into the egg mixture along with the gelatine, which should be put through a strainer.

Now whisk the egg whites—not too stiffly, just to the soft peak stage—and fold them into the mixture gently and carefully. Finally, fold in the whipped cream.

Next pour the mixture into a straight-sided 2 pint (1 litre) soufflé dish, cover and chill for several hours. Serve decorated with blobs—or piped rosettes—of cream and sprinkled with a little grated chocolate.

Baked apple and almond pudding

(serves 4–6 people)

1 lb cooking apples, peeled and sliced (450 g)
2 oz soft brown sugar (50 g)
4 oz ground almonds (110 g)
4 oz butter at room temperature (110 g)
4 oz caster sugar (110 g)
2 large eggs, beaten

Pre-heat the oven to gas mark 4, 350°F (180°C)

A buttered pie dish approximately 1½ pint (850 ml) capacity

Place the apples in a saucepan with the brown sugar and approximately 1 tablespoon water, simmer gently until soft, and then arrange them in the bottom of the prepared pie dish.

In a mixing bowl, cream the butter and caster sugar until pale and fluffy and then beat in the eggs a little at a time. When all the egg is in, carefully and lightly fold in the ground almonds. Now spread this mixture over the apples, evening out the surface with the back of a tablespoon. Then bake on a 'highish' shelf in the oven for exactly 1 hour.

This pudding is equally good served warm or cold—either way it's nice with some chilled pouring cream. It will keep in the refrigerator for 3 or 4 days.

Caramelized apple flan

(serves 4–6 people)

This is from a French recipe called 'Tarte Tatin'—it's baked, chilled and then served upside down.

1 lb cooking or dessert apples, peeled, cored and thinly sliced (450 g)

| 4 oz soft dark brown sugar (110 g) |
| 1 teaspoon ground cinnamon |
| Shortcrust pastry, made with 4 oz plain flour (110 g) and 2 oz butter (50 g) |
| 1 tablespoon melted butter (for greasing) |

Pre-heat the oven to gas mark 4, 350°F (180°C)

An 8 inch (20 cm) sponge tin with no rim and straight sides, brushed with the melted butter, with a circle of greaseproof paper, also brushed with melted butter, covering the base

Begin by covering the base of the prepared tin with brown sugar, pressing it down evenly and well. Now sprinkle on the ground cinnamon, and then arrange the sliced apples neatly, making sure they're pressed well down.

Roll out the pastry to a thickness of approximately $\frac{1}{2}$ inch (1 cm) and cut out a circle that will fit the top of the tin. Cover the apples with the pastry, pressing it down gently. Place in the centre of the oven for 40 minutes until the pastry is golden.

When the tart is quite cold, loosen it round the edges, cover with a plate and carefully turn it all upside down, then remove the tin and the greaseproof paper. Serve with or without cream.

Fruit Crumbles

Crumbles are a good all-round family sweet dish, which can be varied not just by using fruits in season, but also by ringing the changes with the crumble topping. Whatever problems you may have with your pastry-making technique, you're absolutely safe with a crumble because there is no resting or rolling-out involved.

Basic crumble topping

(serves 6 people)

| 8 oz plain flour (225 g) or—and I prefer it—wholewheat flour |
| 5 oz soft brown sugar (150 g) |
| 3 oz butter at room temperature (75 g) |
| 1 level teaspoon baking powder |

Pre-heat the oven to gas mark 4,
350°F (180°C)

Place the flour in a large mixing bowl, sprinkle in the baking
powder, then add the butter and rub it into the flour lightly, using
your fingertips. Then when it all looks crumbly, and the fat has
been dispersed fairly evenly, add the sugar and combine that well
with the rest.

Now sprinkle the crumble mixture all over the fruit in a pie dish,
spreading it out with a fork. Place the crumble on a high shelf in
the oven and bake it for 30–40 minutes or until the top is tinged
with brown.

Variations on the crumble topping
1 Instead of all flour, use 4 oz wholewheat flour (110 g) and 4 oz
jumbo or porridge oats (110 g).
2 Instead of all flour, use 4 oz wholewheat flour (110 g) and 4 oz
muesli (110 g).
3 For a nut crumble topping, use 6 oz (175 g) wholewheat flour
and 3 oz chopped nuts (75 g). You will need to use only 3 oz of soft
brown sugar (75 g) with the 3 oz of butter (75 g).

Spiced apple and raisin crumble

(serves 6 people)

2 lb Bramley apples, peeled and sliced (900 g)
1 oz soft brown sugar (25 g)
¼ teaspoon cloves
1 level teaspoon ground cinnamon
3 oz raisins (75 g)
2 tablespoons water

Pre-heat the oven to gas mark 4,
350°F (180°C)

A 3 pint (1·75 litre) pie dish

Place the sliced apples, raisins, sugar and spices in a saucepan,
sprinkle with the water, then cook gently until the apples are soft
and fluffy. Spoon the mixture into the pie-dish, sprinkle with any
of the crumble toppings (page 694). Use a fork to even it out, but
don't press it down at all. Cook for 30–40 minutes until the
topping is tinged with brown.

Alternative crumble fillings

All the recipes that follow are cooked at the same temperature as the *Spiced apple and raisin crumble* on the previous page and are all cooked in the same size dish (3 pint or 1·75 litre). They all serve 6 people also.

Rhubarb and ginger crumble

Use 2 lb rhubarb (900 g), 3 oz soft brown sugar (75 g) and 1 level teaspoon powdered ginger.

Cut the rhubarb into chunks, then place them in a saucepan together with the sugar and ginger. Cook over a gentle heat (covered) for about 15 minutes, stirring every now and then to get the uncooked pieces at the top down into the heat. Try not to over-cook it, though—it should be chunky rather than mushy. When it's cooked, drain off about half the juice, then transfer the fruit to a pie-dish, sprinkle with one of the crumble toppings (page 694), and bake for 30–40 minutes.

Gooseberry crumble

Use 2 lb gooseberries (900 g) and 6 oz caster sugar (175 g).

Just top and tail the gooseberries, place them in the dish, and sprinkle in the caster sugar. Top straightaway with one of the crumble mixtures (page 694), and bake on the centre shelf of the oven for 40–45 minutes.

Damson (or plum) and cinnamon crumble

Use 2 lb damsons or plums (900 g), 4 oz demerara sugar (110 g) and 1 teaspoon powdered cinnamon.

Wash the damsons or plums, then place them whole in the pie-dish. Sprinkle them with the sugar and cinnamon, then spread with the crumble topping (page 694). I think the nut crumble mixture is the nicest for this. Bake for 30–40 minutes until the topping is tinged with brown. *Note:* plums should be stoned and halved, but damson stones are easier left for the diners to extract!

Dried fruit crumble

For this you can use any combination of dried fruits: prunes, apricots, figs, raisins etc. You need 1 lb mixed dried fruits (450 g), the zest and juice of 1 large orange and 2 oz demerara sugar (50 g).

Soak the fruit overnight in a deep bowl, covered with about $1\frac{1}{4}$ pints (720 ml) of water. Next day drain off $\frac{1}{4}$ pint of the water, then place the rest of the water, the fruit and the sugar in a saucepan, bring to simmering point and simmer for 10 minutes or until the fruit is tender. Then stir in the orange juice and zest, pour the whole lot into the pie dish and top with the basic or the oat crumble (see page 694), and bake for 30–40 minutes.

Blackcurrant crumble

(serves 4–6 people)

1 lb fresh blackcurrants (450 g)
2 tablespoons caster sugar

Pre-heat the oven to gas mark 4, 350°F (180°C)

I think this particular crumble is nicest baked in a shallow 9 inch (23 cm) baking dish (or something similar). Strip the blackcurrants from their stalks, arrange them in the tin, sprinkle with the sugar, top with your choice of crumble (see page 694), and bake for 30–40 minutes.

Raspberry Crumble
This is made in the same way as the blackcurrant crumble, but with 1 instead of 2 tablespoons of caster sugar sprinkled over.

Left-overs

Including recipes for:
Rissoles
Fish cakes
Special cottage pie
Baked, stuffed courgettes
Creamy chicken curry
Ham, egg and cheese risotto
Bubble and squeak
Ham croquettes
Old-fashioned bread pudding

In this, the final part of the Cookery Course, it seemed appropriate to look at what to do with left-overs. However well we plan, and however meticulous we are, we all have food left over at times and it would be criminal not to put it to good use. A recent study in one American city showed that about 15% of the food bought in most households was thrown away—all of it perfectly usable meat, bread and so on. A far cry from the traditional 'Vicarage mutton' which Dorothy Hartley quotes as being served 'hot on Sunday, cold on Monday, hashed on Tuesday, minced on Wednesday, curried on Thursday, broth on Friday, cottage pie on Saturday'.

That must have been quite some joint! But there's a lot to be said for the idea, with the price of meat being what it is. At home, when we do have a joint I like to buy a decent cut, so that it can provide two or three meals. The same goes for poultry or the end of a bacon joint—there's always something that can be made from it.

So here are a few ideas—even for left-over stale bread, which, if you don't own a freezer, can become an enormous problem. Quite simply, make it into an old-fashioned bread pudding, which will disappear in seconds.

Rissoles

My family have a definite weakness for rissoles. We don't eat great quantities of meat, but we *do* have a joint at weekends and that means lots of lovely left-over bits to make rissoles the next day.

The recipe below is my standard one, but in fact the ingredients are by no means invariable. I like to vary them slightly. For something really spicy (with either lamb or beef) I add $\frac{1}{4}$ teaspoon of chilli powder and half a green or red pepper very finely chopped or minced. For a Middle Eastern flavour to your rissoles, try adding $\frac{1}{2}$ teaspoon of ground cumin plus $\frac{1}{2}$ teaspoon ground coriander. Or for an Indian influence, add 1 level teaspoon of curry powder, $\frac{1}{2}$ teaspoon of ginger and $\frac{1}{2}$ teaspoon ground turmeric. Whichever combination you choose, home-made rissoles are delicious!

Rissoles

(serves 2–3 people)

8 oz cooked lamb or beef (225 g)
1 small onion
1½ oz fresh breadcrumbs (40 g)
¼ teaspoon ground cinnamon
2 level tablespoons chopped parsley
1 clove garlic, crushed

| 1 small egg, beaten |
| Salt and freshly-milled black pepper |

For coating and frying:

| Seasoned wholewheat flour |
| Oil, for shallow frying |

Either mince both the onion and the meat through the finest blade of a mincer, or else chop them finely in a food processor. Then place them in a mixing bowl and add the rest of the ingredients. Now just mix and mix until everything is thoroughly blended.

Divide the mixture into six portions, and shape each into a round cake shape with your hands. Then coat each rissole all over with some seasoned wholewheat flour.

All this can be done in advance, and the rissoles can be covered and chilled in the fridge. When you're ready to cook, heat some oil in a frying pan (just enough to cover the base) and when it's very hot, fry the rissoles for 5 minutes on each side.

Fish cakes

(serves 2–3 people)

I think it's actually worth cooking more fish than you need for a meal, just so that you have some left over to make these delicious little fish cakes.

| $\frac{1}{2}$ lb cooked cod (225 g) |
| $\frac{1}{2}$ lb creamed mashed potatoes (225 g) |
| 1 tablespoon chopped parsley |
| $\frac{1}{2}$ teaspoon anchovy essence |
| 1 level teaspoon capers, chopped |
| 1 small egg, beaten |
| $\frac{1}{2}$ oz butter (10 g) (room temperature) |
| 1 teaspoon lemon juice |
| 1 clove garlic, crushed |
| A pinch cayenne pepper |
| A little grated nutmeg |
| Salt and freshly-milled black pepper |

For the coating:

| 1 egg, beaten |
| 3 oz (approx) dry white breadcrumbs (75 g) |

In a large mixing bowl combine all the ingredients for the fish cakes together thoroughly, then taste and season as required with salt and pepper. (If the fish and potatoes are freshly cooked, you will need to chill the mixture at this stage for an hour or two to get it nice and firm.)

When you're ready to cook, lightly flour a working surface, turn the fish mixture out onto it and form it into a long roll 2–2½ inches (5 cm) in diameter. Cut the roll into 12 round fish cakes. Pat each cake into a neat flat shape, and dip each one first into beaten egg and then in the dry white breadcrumbs. Now shallow fry the cakes in equal quantities of oil and butter until golden brown on both sides. Drain on crumpled kitchen paper and serve immediately.

Special cottage pie

(serves 4 people)

This is 'special' because it has a topping of potatoes and leeks which really adds an extra dimension. If you want to make it with raw minced meat, extend the initial cooking time to about 45 minutes (after the stock has gone in) instead of 10 minutes.

1 lb cooked minced beef (450 g)
2 medium-sized onions, chopped
1 large carrot, chopped very small
1 level tablespoon flour
½ teaspoon mixed herbs
½ teaspoon ground cinnamon
1 tablespoon fresh chopped parsley
½ pint hot beef stock (275 ml)
1 tablespoon tomato purée
Some beef dripping
Salt and freshly-milled black pepper

For the topping:
2 lb potatoes (900 g)
2 medium leeks, chopped
2 oz butter (50 g)
Salt and freshly-milled black pepper

Pre-heat the oven to gas mark 6, 400°F (200°C)

First of all fry the onions in the dripping until they are soft, then add the carrot and minced meat, continuing to cook for about 10 minutes until the meat and carrot has browned a little. Now season with salt and pepper and add the cinnamon, mixed herbs and parsley. Stir in the flour, mix the tomato purée with the hot stock, add to the meat mixture and bring to simmering point.

To make the topping: boil the potatoes in salted water and cook the leeks gently in the butter. When the potatoes are done, cream them and then stir in the cooked leeks together with their butter and season to taste.

Put the meat mixture into a well-greased baking dish, spread the potato mixture over the top and bake for about 25 minutes.

Baked stuffed courgettes

(serves 2 people)

This is a Greek-inspired recipe, very good for using up a little left-over lamb.

4 large courgettes
White or brown rice measured to the 3 fl oz level in a measuring jug
1 medium-sized onion, finely chopped
1 clove garlic, crushed
6 oz minced cooked lamb (175 g)
3 tablespoons oil
¼ teaspoon ground cinnamon
1 heaped tablespoon fresh, chopped parsley
12 oz ripe tomatoes, peeled and chopped (350 g)
1 dessertspoon tomato purée
Salt and freshly-milled black pepper

Pre-heat the oven to gas mark 4, 350°F (180°C)

Wipe the courgettes, but don't peel them. Cut each one widthwise into 3 pieces, then using a small knife, flat skewer, or apple corer, hollow out the centre of each piece. You should then end up with 12 hollowed-out little barrel shapes. Now, sprinkle the insides with salt and leave them to drain for about 30 minutes.

While that is happening, cook the rice in double its volume of boiling salted water, until all the water has been absorbed and the rice is grain separate (this will take about 15 minutes for white rice, 40 minutes for brown). Then heat 2 tablespoons of the oil in a frying pan, soften the chopped onion in it for 5 minutes, then stir in the garlic followed by the minced lamb and, finally, the rice. Stir well so that everything gets a good coating of oil. Then sprinkle in the parsley and cinnamon and some seasoning and remove the pan from the heat.

Now wipe the insides of the courgettes with kitchen paper and fill each one with the stuffing, packing it in as tightly as possible. As each one is filled, lay it in a casserole and, when they're all in, tuck any left-over stuffing in between them. Sprinkle another tablespoon of oil all over.

Next beat the tomatoes to a pulp, stir in the tomato purée, season with salt and pepper, and pour the mixture all over the courgettes. Bake with a lid on the casserole for 45 minutes and for a further 15–30 minutes without the lid until the courgettes are tender. Serve with extra rice and perhaps a green salad.

Creamy chicken curry

(serves 4 people)

This is good either for left-over chicken or turkey. It has a fairly mild curry flavour but you can 'hot it up' if you like by adding a little more curry powder.

1 lb cooked chicken, cut into 1 inch (2·5 cm) pieces (450 g)
2 tablespoons groundnut oil
1 large onion, roughly chopped
2 sticks celery, chopped
1 large green pepper, chopped
1 heaped tablespoon flour
1 rounded teaspoon Madras curry powder
1 level teaspoon ginger
1 level teaspoon turmeric
1 pint chicken stock (570 ml)
1 clove garlic, crushed
2 tablespoons double cream
Salt and freshly-milled black pepper

In a large flameproof casserole heat up the oil and soften the onion in it for 5 minutes, then add the chopped celery and green pepper and soften these for 5 minutes more. Next add the prepared chicken pieces and toss them around with the other ingredients.

Now stir in the spices, curry powder and crushed garlic, add the flour and continue to stir to soak up the juices. Next, gradually add the stock, a little at a time, stirring well after each addition. Season with salt and pepper, put a lid on and simmer very gently for 20–25 minutes or until the vegetables are just tender. Remove the curry from the heat, stir in the cream and serve with spiced pilau rice and mango chutney.

Ham, egg and cheese risotto

(serves 3–4 people)

This is a good recipe for using up the remains of a bacon joint.

6 oz boiled bacon, cut into ½ inch (1 cm) cubes (175 g)
Long grain brown rice measured to the ½ pint (275 ml) level in a measuring jug
1 pint boiling water (570 ml)
1½ tablespoons olive oil
2 medium onions, roughly chopped
2 hard-boiled eggs, sliced
2 oz strong Cheddar cheese, grated (50 g)
1 tablespoon breadcrumbs
8 fl oz milk (225 ml)
¾ oz plain flour (20 g)
¾ oz butter (20 g)
Cayenne pepper
Salt and freshly-milled black pepper

In a small flameproof casserole, heat the olive oil and fry the onion for 5 minutes. Then add the bacon cubes, stir in the rice, season with a little salt and pour in the boiling water. Simmer gently— with a lid on—for 45 minutes or until all the water is absorbed and the rice tender.

While that's happening, put the flour, butter and milk in a saucepan, then—whisking continuously—bring to simmering point, by which time the mixture will have thickened. Add a seasoning of salt and freshly-milled black pepper and simmer for 6 minutes. Remove from the heat and stir in half the grated cheese.

A few minutes before the rice is cooked, turn on the grill. Remove the lid from the casserole and, using a skewer, fluff up the rice gently. Then place the sliced eggs over the top and pour on the cheese sauce. Next sprinkle on the rest of the grated cheese and the breadcrumbs and add a dusting of cayenne pepper. Place the dish under a heated grill and serve when the top is brown and bubbly. A fresh crunchy salad goes well with this.

Bubble and squeak

(serves 2 people)

An old-fashioned favourite for using up left-over potatoes and cabbage or you could, of course, use Brussels sprouts.

1 lb cooked potatoes (450 g)
1 small cabbage
1 heaped tablespoon seasoned flour
1 oz butter (25 g)
Beef dripping, for frying
Salt and freshly-milled black pepper

First cut the cabbage into quarters, remove the hard stalk and shred the rest. Wash it thoroughly, then plunge it into fast-boiling water, put a lid on and boil for about 6 minutes. Then transfer the cabbage to a colander and let it drain thoroughly (by putting a plate with a weight on it on top).

Mash the potatoes with the butter and a good seasoning of pepper (preferably with an electric hand whisk). When smooth mix the potatoes with the drained cabbage, then take tablespoons of the mixture and shape them into round cakes. Dust these with seasoned flour, then fry them in hot dripping to a good, crisp, golden brown on both sides. Drain on crumpled greaseproof paper, and serve straightaway.

Ham croquettes

(serves 4 people)

This is obviously a good way to use up left-over ham, but it's also worth buying some ham just to make them.

12 oz cooked ham (350 g)
1 large onion
2 slices wholemeal bread, soaked in a little milk and then squeezed out
1 clove garlic, crushed
1 tablespoon parsley, chopped

2 teaspoons Dijon mustard
1 egg
Some plain flour
Olive oil
Salt and freshly-milled black pepper

Mince the cooked ham, using the coarse blade of your mincer, and put the onion through the mincer also. Then, in a large mixing bowl, combine the ham and onion. Break up the soaked bread and stir this in, together with the garlic, parsley and mustard. Season with pepper, but be sparing with the salt—as the ham may be salty. Add the beaten egg and stir thoroughly.

Now mould the mixture into 8 large—or 12 smallish—croquettes or rolls, pressing firmly to bind them together. Sprinkle some flour onto a pastry board and roll each croquette in it so that they're all lightly dusted with flour. Shallow fry them in olive oil to a light brown colour. Fried eggs make a nice accompaniment.

Old-fashioned bread pudding

(serves 4 people)

This is a lovely spicy cross between a cake and a pudding—perfect for using left-over bread.

8 oz bread (225 g)—it doesn't matter whether this is brown or white but cut off the crusts
½ pint milk (275 ml)
2 oz butter, melted (50 g)
3 oz soft brown sugar (75 g)—if you don't have any brown sugar, you can use white
2 level teaspoons mixed spice
1 egg, beaten
6 oz mixed fruit (175 g)—currants, raisins, sultanas, candied peel
Grated rind of half an orange
Freshly grated nutmeg

Pre-heat the oven to gas mark 4, 350°F (180°C)

A 2–2½ pint (1·25–1·5 litre) baking dish, buttered

Begin by breaking the bread into suitable-sized pieces and place them in a bowl. Pour over the milk, then give the mixture a good stir and leave it for about 30 minutes so that the bread becomes well soaked with the milk.

Now add the melted butter, the sugar, mixed spice and beaten egg. Using a fork, beat the mixture well, making sure that no lumps remain, then stir in the mixed fruit and orange rind. Next spread the mixture in the prepared baking dish and sprinkle over some freshly grated nutmeg. Bake in the pre-heated oven for about $1\frac{1}{4}$ hours. This is nice served with hot custard but some people are particularly partial to eating it cold.

Recommended books

There are so many cookbooks, on every conceivable aspect of cookery, that one hardly knows where to begin. But the following list is a selection of my own favourites, ones which I have found useful. Anyone who has followed the Cookery Course through all three parts should have a working knowledge of the basics of cooking; but for those who want to take the subject further, here is a short list of further reading.

Acton, Eliza *Modern cookery for private families* 1845, reprinted as *The best of Eliza Acton's Modern cookery for private families* by Longman in 1968, and Penguin Books 1980. Several of her recipes have appeared in the Cookery Course.
Carrier, Robert *Food, wine and friends* Sidgwick and Jackson, 1980.
Child, Julia *From Julia Child's kitchen* Cape, n.e. 1978.
Cleave, T. L. *The saccharine disease* Wright, 1974.
Costa, Margaret *Four seasons cookery book* Nelson, 1971; Sphere, 1972.
Duff, Gail *Pick of the crop: cooking with vegetables* Elm Tree Books, 1979.
David, Elizabeth. I have found all her books invaluable. All are published by Penguin Books, and are as follows:
French provincial cooking 1970; *French country cookery* 1970; *Italian food* 1970; *Mediterranean food* 1970; *Salt, spices and aromatics in the English kitchen* vol. 1 of *Ancient and modern English cooking* 1970 and *English bread and yeast cookery* 1980.
Grigson, Jane *The International Wine and Food Society's guide to fish cookery* David and Charles, 1973; Penguin Books, 1975. *The vegetable book* Michael Joeseph, 1978; Penguin Books, 1980.
Hartley, Dorothy *Food in England* Macdonald, 1955; paperback 1975. The standard reference work on the subject.
Hazan, Marcella *The classic Italian cook book* W. H. Allen, 1975.
Home and freezer digest *Will it freeze?* Jill Norman, 1980.
Leith, Prue and Waldegrave, Caroline *Leith's cookery course* (3 vols) Fontana, 1980.
Liddell, Caroline *The wholefood cook book* Coronet, 1980.
Loewenfeld, Claire *Herb gardening* Faber, 1964.
Lyon, Ninette *Meat at any price* Faber, paperback 1969.
Ministry of Agriculture *Home preservation of fruit and vegetables* HMSO, 1972.

Rubinstein, Helge and Bush, Sheila *Ices galore* Deutsch, 1977.
Smith, Delia. More of my own recipes may be found in the
following books all published by Coronet:
How to cheat at cooking 1973; *Frugal food* 1976; *The 'Evening Standard'
cook book* 1978 and *Delia Smith's Book of cakes* 1978. Other recipes
from some of the leading restaurateurs in England can be found in
Recipes from country inns and restaurants Ebury Press, 1973. op.
Smith, Michael *Fine English cookery* Faber, 1977.
Stewart, Katie *'The Times' cookery book* Collins, 1972,
and *'The Times' calendar cook book* Pan, 1977.
Stobart, Tom *Herbs, spices and flavourings* Penguin Books, n.e. 1977.
Tovey, John *Entertaining with Tovey* Macdonald and Jane's, 1979.

Index